THE
CWORD

BEING CHOSEN AS A VESSEL
FOR
GOD'S MODERN CANCER MIRACLE

AIRAM BATDORF

To my husband, Michael-

We never expected the calling on our journey, but I am
forever grateful it has been with you. From trench to trench
and peak to peak, I will always love you.
Our love pushed me to fight.
I deeply thank you. I respect you. I cherish you.

To my mom-

Thank you for all you have done and all your support.
I always hope to make you proud.

And, to you Lord-

Here I am.

AKB

CONTENTS

PART 1 1

CHAPTER 1 2

CHAPTER 2 9

CHAPTER 3 16

CHAPTER 4 20

CHAPTER 5 32

CHAPTER 6 38

CHAPTER 7 50

CHAPTER 8 57

CHAPTER 9 67

CHAPTER 10 74

CHAPTER 11 80

CHAPTER 12 93

CHAPTER 13 101

CHAPTER 14 115

PART 2 130

PART 1

CHAPTER 1

My husband Michael was out of town moving my sister-in-law into her new apartment; they were driving her things from Chicago to New York. I remember when they were making this trip it was still the dead of winter. That night they were driving through a huge snowstorm. In hindsight, I remember thinking, "He has no idea we're both in a storm." Mine was rather different. It was a normal day, or so I thought.

I went to the gym that morning. After I came home, I started to make some oatmeal on the stove. I had some gospel music going on in the background while standing at the stove, giving it a stir when needed so it wouldn't overflow everywhere. I stood at the stove with my right foot on my left calf, and I had the spoon in my mouth, scrolling with my other hand on my iPhone. Doing a quick scroll through Facebook, there was an article that popped up and it was about a young woman who was around 30 years old. She was featured in New York Fashion Week; bold, black, beautiful, and I was stunned by her presence that radiated through the phone. They had her walk down the runway with a sheer shirt on because due to her double mastectomy- which means to completely remove the entire breast- she didn't have any nipples. At that present moment, many things were shocking to me. First, it was her strength. The second shock factor was confusion; I'm not kidding, literal shock. Never, in my whole life had I ever heard of any woman under the age of 50 or 60 getting breast cancer. I remember being floored; I had just seen something I had never even known existed. Here was this young woman like a fiery gazelle giving her testimony. It was bold; I naturally gravitate towards bold. I was inspired, eagerly intrigued and captivated, almost as if something supernatural was prompting my curiosity to press forward.

I clicked to find her Instagram and the first video I clicked on was of her humbly advocating in her home for young women to self check their breasts, even if they had no cancer history in their family. "You're never too young to self check your breasts," she went on to say. She was 27 when she found her lump and was diagnosed. I was 27 at the time. I, to this day, on everything I love, will never be able to fully describe such a moment that was both eerie and divine. My stomach immediately felt sick, I felt my back get hot as I lifted my right arm up. The hairs on my arm and neck were standing up. I looked forward and I couldn't see or hear anything else in the room. There was a whisper that appeared in this slow motioned, oddly panicked moment that gently said, "Check your breasts." I've learned so intimately that God speaks in whispers. However, I didn't want to. What if something was there? *Why am I sweating?*

I put the spoon and phone down. I, at this point in my life, had never, ever self-checked my breasts. I've only had a doctor feel them a couple times during a physical exam. Besides, who checks them at 27? That's absurdly young in my mind. A little background: I have zero cancer history on either side of my family. Cancer, or what I soon called the C-word, was only something other people got. A thought has never crossed my mind that it could be me or would possibly be me. Right in that moment I felt my breasts, unsure of how to properly check. I gently pushed a little deeper, and there it was. My heart started to pound and my hands turned cold inside like when you start to panic. There was a hard lump, tucked deeply in my right breast. My left breast didn't have that. *"Why doesn't my left boob have this? Why is it hard? What is that?"* I had a supernatural feeling within my spirit. Without having a knowing, I knew.

My oatmeal foamed all over the stove.

Our Coincidence Is His Orchestration

I used to call it irony or coincidence, but it's really all God's orchestration. That feeling of *knowing* is largely attributed to how I had been led to find it. I knew it was Him. I'm constantly in awe at the depths that He intertwines, moves, shapes and shifts things on levels we will never comprehend. We physically cannot comprehend them. And yet, somehow, they all work together for our good. What was "ironic," was that my mother-in-law had breast cancer the year before. She surprised my husband at our wedding in Mexico because she wasn't going to be able to make it due to her lumpectomy date. I knew Mikey was crushed, but he's brave. I've learned that a lot of my bravery is learned from him. It's a great memory in our family. Furthermore, her mom, Michael's grandma, also had breast cancer, and likewise his grandma's sister passed away from breast cancer. Although we aren't blood related, I believe God graciously "paired" me with a family that had been where I was going to go; they were living testimonies for me to believe. Almost like a graceful gift from God. They were allies in my loneliness at times. Above all else, they fully believed it was God who healed them. They're great people of faith. I know my earth family wasn't an accident.

When I felt the lump I called my mother-in-law right away, literally that next minute. My heart was racing and as she picked up, I said, "Mom, I'm freaking out. I think I feel a lump in my right breast and I'm afraid it's..." If you know my mother-in-law, she's calm. I started literally rambling about the 20 minute sequence of events that had supernaturally led me to find the lump in the first place and she calmly interjected. "Airam, it's okay. Call your doctor and make an appointment. I'm sure it's not that but it's good to get it checked so that you'll be sure and you won't be worried."

Do you know when sales people or commercials say, "Wait! There's more!" You're going to feel like that a lot within this story because it happens over, and over, and over again. Starting with the way I found the lump in the first place; let me backup a few months. When I found the lump, it was at the end of February 2018. A few short months before that in December it was open enrollment for insurance. See, my husband and I had been striving entrepreneurs for years. We met in corporate but neither of us were really cut out for that world; we had side businesses and Michael had worked his butt off, ramping up a successful gutter cleaning company here in Washington. (*Mikey, I'm so proud of you! Just want to tell you*). The life of the great unknown in entrepreneurship, however, meant that we didn't have benefits, which meant we didn't have health insurance for a long while.

We honestly never felt we needed it. We were young, healthy, and never sick, never injured; ate relatively good and worked out every day with no previous health alarms. It was December and my mom brought up that open enrollment was about to end at the end of the month. She was persistent about us getting it since we were about to go into our second year of marriage - (*she's Filipino, we're often persistent people*). "What if you want to have a baby?" she asked. We were actually planning on that for 2018. It's crazy how much life can change from our plans. "What if one of you gets sick? Or hurt? You're making enough money now where the extra $500 a month won't break you guys. This is important," she insisted. Don't get me started with the absurd cost and yet eye opening importance for insurance, but my gratitude in this story of God's grace highly trumps it. Here's the "irony" again. We ended up taking her advice. We signed up for health insurance on the very last enrollment day while driving in the middle of nowhere in the pitch dark while doing an exposure for business late at night. It was at the final hour, barely getting reception and desperately trying to find an app on my phone that would "fax" the information the agent needed. By human standards I have no clue how she received it but in the supernatural realm, slam dunk! (*Anyone know what I'm talking about? "If ya don't know, now ya know." Come on Biggie! Ok, back to finding the lump*).

Our insurance became active six weeks before I found the lump. Six weeks. We hit the deductible in *one* appointment if that puts into perspective how much of a blessing it was. To paint an even clearer picture: when I found the lump, we didn't even have our insurance cards and no insurance ID numbers that we knew of. In fact, I literally had to quickly rummage through the house to find the packet that would remind me which insurance company we were even with. Which means, how the heck do I call the doctor when I don't have a doctor? I had no clue where to locate the doctor's office or even where to call. I'm not joking when I say I called the 1-800 number to my insurance and said, "I don't know if you can help me but I was just making my oatmeal and I found a lump in my breast. I don't fully know if my insurance is even activated, I don't have an ID number, but I can give you my name and I need to see a doctor ASAP." Needless to say, after about 40 minutes of detective work and transfers, I finally got to someone that said:

"Mrs. Batdorf, there's a clinic nearby and it's actually only 10 minutes away from you! Would you like me to transfer you?"

"Yes."

The front office proceeded, "Mrs. Batdorf, this absolutely never happens but we had a cancellation today and it's in 2 hours. Would you like to come in?"

"YES!"

CHAPTER 2

Remember how my hubby was driving through a snow storm? Now you see how the both of us were in our own storms. I'll never forget stopping for a second and comprehending what I had just made an appointment for but telling myself *it's nothing*. I needed to call him because I had no idea how insurance worked, but was prepared to pay whatever was needed to make sure this wasn't anything.

I called him, rolled my shoulders back, and put a smile on so it would transfer through the phone. "Hey babe!" Hearing Mikey's voice that morning warmed me and for some reason broke me at the same time. I could feel his love and smile across the phone as he shared about his day and vividly told me how crazy the snow storm was. He shared how him and his sister were having a great time bonding and were stopping for some good food. "What's up, how's your day babe?" he asked. I said, "It's going good! Just holding down the fort over here, eating some breakfast. Hey, I need to run to the doctor's office today. It's TOTALLY nothing to worry about but I just wanted to let you know in case you see a charge on our bank account."

I was scared...and alone. He on the other hand was experiencing a new memory with his sister that I was so excited for. I wished he was home but I didn't feel the timing was by any accident at all. I closed my eyes and held the phone with two hands and imagined hugging him. He was confused. You know when you love someone so much you want to protect them? I felt an inherent obligation to protect Mikey. As strong-willed and unshakeable as he is on the outside, he has a tender heart and is my big baby. He was my sweetheart. My new husband. I didn't want to share what my worry was or what I had just discovered. I didn't want to burden or have him worrying on his trip with his sister. It could wait, which is so like me. I'm an empathetic; I will always carry something for someone which is one of my greatest strengths in some ways and a downfall in others. With everything that had happened with his mom recently, it was a sensitive spot and too close to home for us to ever imagine. And, he was thousands of miles across the country. It wasn't going to change anything in that moment if he knew. What good was it going to do for me to tell him? I told myself it was better to wait.

"The doctors? Are you ok? What's going on?" His voice changed.

"Oh babe, really. It's nothing, I promise! I'll tell you when you get home. Don't worry."

I forced myself to buck up and sound extra assuring, with extra energy and a smile.

"Well, ok, if you say so! I love you. Call me later."

It's crazy how much of a moment stays tucked away in our memory. I can be typing this while sitting in a coffee shop and have my eyes filled with tears because I can still see and feel everything around me as if I'm still living in that moment. I travel back in time and I see us: me at the house and him across the country, like two kids with no clue as to what God was going to lead them through in their innocence. I say "them" because for those of you who are married, you know that this is a "we" thing. It's not just one of you that goes through the highs and lows of life. It's both of you. For some reason, thinking of those two newlyweds breaks me. I'm grateful that I know the end of the story though. So hang on with us.

The Holy Spirit Intervenes

At this point, the only person who knew anything about this possible situation was my mother-in-law. I proceeded to call my best friend because I was so nervous about going to this appointment alone. I couldn't believe how fast things were happening. *(This is still the same day I found the lump!)* I was feeling relieved and scared at the same time. She, being the type of friend she is, dropped what she was doing and came. We got to the parking lot of the clinic and we said a quick prayer. We checked in, I got called back, and my best friend came into the room with me. There was no way I was going in there alone.

The doctor seemed pretty relaxed and had a demeanor like, *"What do we got goin' on here,"* in a super light fashion. She asked me some questions that I distinctly remember feeling as though she was intentionally trying to point to this lump being nothing. Kind of like when you're in court and they ask you questions on purpose to make the verdict appear different from your case. "Any previous health history? Anyone in your family ever had any sort of health issues? Any cancer in your family? Do you work out? I see you have a fancy Fit-Bit watch and athletic clothes. You must workout a lot. That's good! You're how old again? Only 27?" I could hear the, "*Oh this is nothing*" in her head.

It annoyed me. Not because she was upbeat, but because I felt the upbeat energy was actually a, "*there's no reason for you to be here.*" It belittled my feelings and concern that were clearly evident. Shouldn't we want to encourage people not to be ashamed or afraid when they're concerned about their body? Shouldn't we feel safe and that doctors are on our side? In that moment, I wondered how many people could have found what was wrong with them much earlier but didn't go to a doctor's office for this very reason.

She had me remove my shirt, lay down on the table so she could do a breast exam with her hands to feel the lump I was talking about. I always thought this was so awkward when I was younger. You lay with your hands above your head and they massage your boobs while keeping conversation, kind of like at the dentist. But at the dentist is actually worse because you can't even respond. I never understood that. She was still peppy in her demeanor and gave a couple, "hmm"s. "Ok, yeah I do feel that," she said. "Cancer normally feels much harder than this." She handed me my shirt and I sat up holding it with my arms crossed to cover myself. She continued, "You know, normally we don't advise young women at your age to self check their breasts because women your age are hormonal and lumps are completely normal. It can make them paranoid. It's a good idea to just come back next year for your physical. You're far too young, way too healthy and have no history with you or anyone in your family to worry about. I do think it is a bit over-reactive."

PSA: to be crystal clear, this is horrible advice.

Over-reactive? I think she meant for that to comfort me. *Over-reactive*, she said. I'll never forget looking at my best friend's face, her mouth slightly opened, filled with anger and confusion that said, *what the heck* (but with a much more vulgar word). I could tell she was in mama bear mode. Although I'm sure the doctor intended in good nature to downplay what the situation was so I wouldn't worry, it truthfully made me feel like an idiot for possibly thinking this was cancer. I mean, who wouldn't feel like an idiot? It made me feel like I was stupid for even coming to the doctor, speaking up, or relaying my concern. It made me feel, "over-reactive" and like Paranoid Patty.

I felt more discouraged than before, actually. In hindsight, however, I was very angry. First off, hold the freaking phone. No doctor should ever make you feel stupid for coming to see them to check something you are concerned about. This is their job. I'll talk about this later in the book, but if your doctor does do this, do like I did – get a new doctor. Second, remember that divine God prompting that overtook me when I felt led to even check my breasts in the first place? It came back and it came with heat.

To set the record straight: In knowing myself, I am the type of person where if a doctor, (who's the professional here people), told me I was fine I would just go with it. Especially in a case like this where the obvious verdict you're hoping for is a whopping, "You're in the clear! Definitely not that. Nada. Zip. Who wants coffee? Or a drink?" But this time was different. When she told me it was nothing, my spirit jumped out of my bones and out came this person. I sat up a little straighter, I looked at my best friend, and I looked back at the doctor dead in her eyes. The Holy Spirit paired with my inherent boldness ended up daringly saying, "My husband and I pay $500 a month for insurance now. Unless you can tell me 100% this is not cancer, I need you to schedule me for whatever test you need to." *Silence.* The Holy Spirit was making a debut ya'll. My gaze on her never broke.

"Well, can you?"

She stammered. She was thrown off her normal balance in her practice of keeping it routine and seeing people with clogged ears and rashes. I wasn't backing down, and neither was my intuition. She said, "Well, no. Of course I can't tell you this isn't cancer by just feeling it and doing a physical examination."

Silence again.

"I'll send a referral for you to get an ultrasound." In hindsight, I like to envision my guardian angels in the room standing behind me with their arms crossed and in front of her saying, "*Yeah, that's right.*" Just maybe.

CHAPTER 3

Mikey made it back from New York and I was so relieved to have him home. The very first thing he asked me after a kiss and a normal *hello* was a sweet but abrupt demand to tell him what the doctor's appointment was all about. I told him what happened: I had found a lump and that only his mom, our friend and he knew. I told him about the appointment. I told him I already had the ultrasound scheduled. We both honestly just kind of acted like it was nothing. I guess this is just our DNA individually and as a couple.

We always believe in the positive. We adamantly don't give energy to the negativity within our household. The basis of our morals and beliefs open a small window into how I naturally approached this journey. I wasn't always this way. When I met my husband, he was like nothing I had ever seen before: Relentlessly demanding of the best in life, didn't believe in quitting, filled with assurance and energy. He had aggressive tenacity, drive and positivity. He was the first person that I had personally witnessed have that much drive towards self betterment and chasing dreams. I never grew up around this. Not that my parents or the people I grew up with were bad people, but my upbringing was void of many of Mikey's characteristics. Although oddly, he is a clone of my dad and my brother in many ways. I just wasn't actually raised that way. I had never heard of personal development until I met Michael Batdorf at the ripe age of just 23. He was turning 30. I look back and think of myself as a baby still at that age.

A Young Me

I knew I was different than most people. I had huge potential and was (am) talented, but lost, unsure of myself on the inside, and without any real foundation other than trying to be the tough independent woman. I've always had an old soul, a dreamer spirit and a knowing since I was very young that one day I was going to have a huge influence on many. I just had no idea how. Mikey was the bridge. He was like an energizer bunny with all the setting modes of Gary Vaynerchuk, Eric Thomas and Tony Robins turned *ON*. You can imagine he's a lot to handle as his wife. As nuts as he is, I was deeply drawn to him as if God chose him for me and I had no say. *I was happy with God's choice.* I mean, it was like a scene out of a movie: Mutual love at first sight. Mikey and I didn't know God when we first met. But, as God is Almighty, He bumped us together and it's evident in hindsight why. We grew to truly find God individually for the first time and build our faith together. There's His orchestration again. My world went upside down, or rather more like right side up, because the little girl in me that knew since she was younger that she was going to be something huge in this world had finally met someone that matched a frequency she knew she had but didn't know how to find. It seemed like my actual normal that had been denied for so many years. A part of me that was always there and belonged was making a debut.

Mikey and I met in the sales industry and have been in the direct sales industry together throughout our entire relationship. We've attempted and started big ideas and businesses individually and together. Our journey was always filled with ambition and crazy dreams; two kids jumping from cloud to cloud. Mikey introduced me to the idea that I actually could do anything I wanted and anything I believed. There was nothing or no one that could stop that. If you knew Mikey and I's individual history, you'd understand why we both gravitated towards this and each other. Personal development, self mastery, inclusion and motivation are the cellular building blocks within that world. And I love it.

Meeting Mikey, leading to the industries we were in, leading to the direction of my life and how I wanted to live it, were like the tiny seeds that were planted within and for each other. They taught me things like how to work towards self-actualization, the power of our thoughts, the power of our words, habits as building blocks to success from finances to emotions; to reading books that would shape me to be the best version of myself, how to understand what success takes and what kind of person achieves at a high level. And, it introduced me to so many authors, speakers, and leaders that I would look to as an example at how to be an overcomer, a do'er, an impactor, and an all around badass.

It was almost as if this realm raised me as a young woman. I'd read a ton of books, listened to countless podcasts, audios and talks on YouTube, went to at least seven different trainings or seminars each year, and purposefully surrounded myself around people who were empowering, uplifting and aligned with these goals and direction. These things taught me how to focus my outer self, my inner being, my outer world, and to know that a circumstance is just a circumstance. They taught me the principle to truly not give up and to fight in the ring of life. It gave me an approach.

CHAPTER 4

So, now that Mikey knew, the next appointment was the ultrasound. This was my first time going to the actual hospital where there was a whole breast care center. I'd soon find I would become pretty familiar with that place. There were bulletin boards with how to check your breasts, statistics and posters that would have motivational imagery and quotes. There were light pink ribbons everywhere and most of the nurses had lanyards with pink ribbon pins on them. They called me back and the nurse looked at me and double checked her chart. You could tell her thoughts: "She looks way too young. Is she the right person?" I mean I'll be honest. I've looked younger than my age my whole life. I'm half Filipino and half Guatemalan and Spanish, with a few other neat ethnicities. The older I get the more I find pride in saying I age like fine wine. I hated it when I was younger but pushing 30, I love it now. Thanks mom! But, it didn't evade from the fact that baby face or not, 27 was way too young for anyone to really think the possibility of the cancer was normal, even for those who worked within that line of work.

<u>The Calm Before The Storm</u>

She took me back and showed me where I would undress, told me to put a gown on, and to wait for the technician to come get me. I pulled the curtain to shut it, took my tops off and looked at myself in the mirror. I looked myself dead in the eyes and I said, "You're going to be okay."

I pulled the curtain back, and I sat down. The technician came and brought me to the back left room. They had the lights dimmed, which was actually comforting. She told me to lay down and show her where the lump was. After putting cold gel on me, she started moving the ultrasound tool around my breast. I had my face slightly turned while staring at a spot I had picked on the ceiling. I was talking to God and telling myself I was okay. She said, "Oh okay, here it is. I'm just going to take a few images and then the radiologist will come in and chat with you real quick okay?" She was sweet. I sat in there by myself until the radiologist came in. She explained to me that what they were looking for was to see if this lump was filled with fluid or solid. Mine was solid. But, she assured me this was common and for me not to worry. With no history in my family, my health history, my age and just what they've seen before, she was calmly reassuring me that this would more than likely be benign. However, they would want to do a biopsy to be sure. I wanted to believe her.

About a week and a half later it was time to do the biopsy. Mikey stayed out in the waiting room. I remember tearing up before this appointment. Thinking back, this moment was the first I remember experiencing real fear. I mean when they said, "we are going to need a tissue sample of what's in there," all I could think about was, "*Well, how the heck do you get in there?*" Second, there were only two verdicts to this test. It either wasn't cancer or it was. I asked my mother-in-law what a biopsy was like. She told me it hurt but that it wasn't as bad as she thought it would be. It gave me some comfort to find out the procedure wasn't as drastic as I imagined. Googling what it was going to be like never sounded like a good idea. I wanted to just expect good and have no influences making me think otherwise. Plus, I didn't want to unnecessarily freak myself out. I never googled one procedure of mine. I headed into the doctor's office in expectation that everything was going to be fine.

My biopsy was at the same hospital, same breast center, and actually the same exact room as the ultrasound. The original radiologist who looked at my ultrasound was going to be the one to do it and I remember it was an unfortunate and sweet "Hello, again" but still hopeful. She explained what they were going to need to do but before she even started talking, my eyes were looking at the tools on the medical table. I rolled my shoulders back and told myself *this wasn't anything I couldn't handle*. Why do tools always look so much more dramatic than they are? She explained that they were going to cut an incision on my breast, then use the ultrasound to guide this huge needle looking thing into my breast to where the lump was. This thing worked like a toy. It was a hollow tube and when she pushed this button, it would make the needle shoot out and grab a tissue sample from the lump. All I remember was how loud it was; it sounded like a staple gun. While laying on the table, I picked a spot on the ceiling again and remember saying to myself, "*you're brave, you're strong; God's got you. You're doing great, Airam.*" I felt God saying to me, "Just focus."

One of my best friends loves to tell me that one of my spiritual gifts is that God talks to me in such a unique way and a lot of it is in these intricate, imaginative visuals. They're powerful, supernatural and vivid. During the cancer journey there were a lot of visualizations I'd find myself in. One was in the ocean and another was in the boxing ring. The unexpected is always difficult because, well, you didn't expect it. You couldn't calculate how to hear it. You couldn't plan how to react or avoid the situation. You couldn't pray ahead or personally develop yourself spiritually or mentally for this exact situation. You couldn't physically prepare to have the wind taken out of you, and you couldn't anticipate the fall, devastation, fear, or pain. It's a shock-factor.

There is no easy way to get the crap knocked out of you. If you knew it was coming, you wouldn't have gotten the crap knocked out of you.

You understand what I mean? There is no comfortable way to get the upper cut or perfect punch that whirls you in a half circle and lands you on the floor with your face to the side. In the slow motion of the fall, you see sweat and blood in the air. There just isn't anything that can help you plan for the unexpected. You can only react to the punch.

I was 27 when I was diagnosed with breast cancer. I had been married to my sweetheart and best friend for only about a year and a half. The whole world was at my feet. We were good people, happy with big spirits, highly ambitious, truly loved each other and loved the Lord. This was not in the plan. We all say that, don't we?

Surpassing Understanding

When I got the call, I had been anxiously waiting for three days after my biopsy. I was wrapped in a blanket in the fetal position by our fireplace where I spent a lot of time trying to meditate and just talk to God. It was this cheesy blanket that had Mikey and I's engagement picture on it with our dog Brody. One of our good friends got it for us as a wedding gift. The doctors told me that the latest I would find out from the biopsy was the third day, and it was 4:30PM on the last day they said they would call. They were closing soon, and I immediately knew they waited until the end of their day to call me to deliver the news. I wondered how they must have gone to one another after seeing the report, wondering who was going to give me the call. *How should we make the call? How do we tell her that this is actually cancer when we were all so sure that it wasn't?* In the first two words, "Hi, Airam?" I knew what the news was by the questioning and heavy tone.

Knockout.

She was slow to speak. She told me that the results said it was cancer. I'm sure she had delivered this type of news countless times before, but her voice was still humanly very somber. It was hesitant. It was afraid. It was sympathetic. I remember her saying, "I'm so sorry. We really did not believe this was going to be the outcome." I believed her, but her voice started to go out in my mind.

She paused, and said the good news was that it was Stage 1 and non-aggressive from what they can see. She cleared her throat and I could tell she forced herself to pick up the momentum a little; she remembered she had a job as a doctor and continued to talk while throwing some jargon in there. I walked into the bathroom and looked at myself in the mirror, rolled my shoulders back and took a deep breath. It might have been the shock but not one tear fell. After I somewhat floated back down, I hadn't noticed that although I was somewhere else, my voice was saying "ok" very calmly to her throughout her spiel.

I finally cut her off and said, "*What's next?*" in my business voice. I walked down the steps, picked up a picture frame of Mikey and I smiling ear to ear on our wedding day, and then made my way to the kitchen. She took a moment, and meekly replied, "I understand this is difficult, but I'm not quite sure you're hearing me." I don't know if it was that she was used to people reacting hysterically, or if she was weirded out by my probably eerie calm, but I could tell she was incredibly thrown off. She stammered, regained composure and she kept pushing me to watch a video explaining what breast cancer was and that she was going to send it to my email. I knew she was shocked that I was calm. I was shocked too, but at the same time wasn't. It felt peculiarly natural and Déjà vu like.

I cut her off again, "Ma'am, I hear you. I really do. But, what's next? Who do I need to see and when is the next available appointment?" She explained it wasn't that simple to just book the next appointments and she then resorted back to insisting I watch the video. That stupid video. To this day I never watched it; it remains an unopened email deep in the abyss.

I do have a lot of grace for this woman. She did her best with news no one wants and it wasn't her fault. But I chose to receive the news differently. I could accept the news with God's very supernatural power, but I wasn't going to just accept this as my "fate." It never felt like that. There was something that was strongly stirring in me in the spiritual realm that it was okay to be calm. See, I did hear what she was saying. I wasn't sitting there saying, "No she didn't say that. That's not what she said. She's lying." But there was something much louder drowning her out.

It was a resounding, overwhelming peace I couldn't explain. Something physically blanketed me in my entirety and it was oddly comforting. There was a quiet voice saying, "Airam, I know you hear what you're hearing. But listen to me.

I need you to trust me. Everything is going to be OK." In my faith, I could hear God a lot in various ways, but not like this. I later learned this was a first hand experience with what God says He'll supernaturally give us through the Holy Spirit. A supernatural peace that surpasses all understanding (Philippians 4:7) and an all-powerful loud voice from Him in the form of an incredibly gentle whisper. Peace that surpasses understanding is beautifully illogical. It overtook me, took the reigns of my thoughts and held me safely while hearing what I was hearing in the "here."

She told me my assigned nurse was going to call me and we hung up. I put the phone down and looked out the window. I put my hand over my mouth as it was uncontrollably trembling. Time stopped, I had a long blink, and there it came. I opened my eyes and they were violently flooding with tears. My top half of my body caved in and very slowly bent over with both my hands over my mouth. I let out a primal wail. I was down for the count: Motionless, face on the side of the mat, and the ref had counted to 10.

The Storm

I remember my first thoughts were that this couldn't be real, and then I thought about my husband. My heart broke. I haltingly turned around to look at the rest of our place and it was as if everything was in slow motion and it all of a sudden felt like I was in a totally different world. A familiar scene but in a weird dream. I couldn't breathe and was begging God while panicking to overtake my body before I thought it was going to literally burst at every seam. I was drowning. This was my first imagery of the water. I was in a huge, open abyss in the ocean, kicking and paddling fiercely, again, in slow motion. The sky was black, the water was deep blue, and there were only flashes from the storm. My face was in pure anguish, I could see the bubbles from me yelling underwater and I was being pulled deeper, and deeper, and deeper.

Michael was on the roof doing a job in a neighborhood not too far from us. I called him immediately and he didn't answer. I called my best friend next and she picked up. There were no words, just hard sobs and trying to breathe. She told me to slow down and all I said was, "the doctor called." There was a long pause, and all she said was, "I'm coming." Mikey called back quickly after that and I in a panic said, "Mikey...you need to come home right now." He said, "What is it?" I was looking out the window again and just cried. We were both silent and I could hear his breathing become heavier. No other words needed to be said. "I'm coming right now." He abruptly left mid-job. I dropped to my knees, and I let out another wail. The odd peace was still there in my spirit, but my human self and body were trying their best to process something so intense. I lifted my head, looked straight ahead with steel eyes, covered my face, wiped my tears and I got up. Forcefully pacing from my kitchen to my living room back and forth, I told myself to breathe deep. The only thing my instinct could think to do was repeatedly say, "The Lord is my Shepard. He makes me lie down in green pastures. He leads me beside still waters; I will fear no evil. He will never forsake me (Psalms 23)." Over, and over, and over again. Each time I got louder with the tone being: "*God come down RIGHT NOW! God please save me from myself at this moment. Don't leave me.*" There was anger, then urgency, then faith, then shock, then sorrow, then hope, looping and looping. I'd stop in my tracks for a split second with a silent cry and then start pacing again doing the only thing I knew to do to keep me relatively calm.

Mikey's truck zoomed into the driveway and I started to walk towards the garage door. He came upstairs quickly, we looked at each other, and I ran into his arms. He had his hands on my face, panicked, trying to lift my face from his chest asking me to please talk to him and tell him what happened. My face was still buried, and I said, "They said that it's cancer." He grabbed me by the shoulders and forcefully pulled me just a little away from him so that I'd have to look at him. "Are you being serious?" My eyes were so wet, my cheeks were hot, and I looked at him with soft eyes, and a gentle broken smile. "Yes, babe."

Mikey and I sat on the floor together, and if you ask both of us, this was the only time in the whole journey we remember us really crying together. He sat with his back against the couch and I was on his lap facing him. He cried, and he said "It shouldn't be you. Why is it you? It should be me. It's not supposed to be you. This isn't supposed to happen to you." I stopped crying and I felt a strong pull inside of me. I immediately leaned back a little, I grabbed him by the face, and

I remember sternly saying, "Hey. Look at me. This is not supposed to be you. God chose me. And I don't know how to explain this, but *I. Am. Going. To. Be. Okay.* Do you hear me?" We stared into each other's eyes, our souls saying to each other, "I'm scared." We sat for about 30 minutes just crying, holding each other and not speaking. I was still straddling him with our arms around each other, my face turned to the side on his shoulder and he finally said, "You're going to beat this." I said, "I know."

I share this part in-depth, as vulnerable and raw as this is, because I see you. Your "C-word" could be cancer, the way you heard your diagnosis, heard you lost a child, heard your spouse say they were leaving or had an affair, got the eviction notice or had your dream snatched. Whatever "C-word" in your life laid the punch, it may look different than my experience, but it felt the same. You need to know that from experience, I see you, I hear you, and I know how you must feel. And you are not alone.

There are things in life that will happen that are difficult to accept. There will be some things we don't want, certainly would never choose, and there will be others that are genuinely too painful to swallow. They hurt so bad that it's almost as if our body physically rejects it. It feels immeasurable in the initial moment, and for however long after, you feel immobilized. There will be things that will happen to you that you don't deserve. They won't make sense, and sometimes there won't be an explanation we can understand. Everyone is different in how they may manage their response to these things, but we are all the same in that we cannot evade things happening. It's life. And remember, it in fact does not mean God does not love you. But rather that He has an opportunity to show how mighty He is to heal, renew, strengthen, and exemplify His grace and love for you. He has nothing to prove to us, but it gives us a chance to see proof that He really is who He says He is. It might be in our health, our relationships, our family, our finances, or our dreams; These are simply avenues for our soul to find Him. It hurt for me. And it hurt for us, as a family. But we knew this was not an end. It was the very beginning of a journey.

CHAPTER 5

I gained a whole new perspective to acceptance in this experience. In looking up the definition of the word accept, it says to "believe or come to recognize as valid or correct." Here's the thing: When circumstances happen to us, there is a "here and now" perspective, and there is an "above" perspective. The "here and now" perspective is what you experience, see, hear and feel externally or internally and emotionally. The "above" perspective is looking at what God is orchestrating. It takes not only consideration but faith and declaration of who He was, who He is, what He does and what His nature is. The God who loves you more than you could ever possibly imagine and works for your good. What might it look like from "up there," where you aren't limited to the viewpoint of what is simply in front of you and your human abilities?

See, as humans, we don't have the physical capacity to fully understand God's supernatural abilities, nature, or divine orchestration. We physically can't fully understand the amount of love He has for us. When we ask God questions, more often than not we wouldn't be able to even remotely comprehend the answers because they are so complex, supernatural and vast. They wouldn't make sense to us and it would be too much to handle grasping. We would implode trying to fathom. That's why He graciously guides us and gives us little by little. So, I looked at the "here and now" but I also knew there was a much larger picture from "up there." And, He gave me just enough to know and have supernatural peace to trust Him.

Fact: There was a lump I could feel in my breast. Fact: The biopsy resulted that it was the cancer. Was I denying that the test results came back the way they did? No. Was it valid and correct that the diagnosis was cancer? Yes. Did I tell the doctors they were wrong and they were liars? No. Did I recognize that I was going to go down the options and treatment path whether I was ready, wanted to, or could catch my thoughts that, "This is where we're at?" Yes. These were things I wasn't in denial about.

From Now On, It's The C-word

Sometimes, however, there is no way to explain how you know what you know. Maybe it's like when some of us know our soulmate by the first eye-lock, or how I read once in a book called, *Blue Like Jazz*, that Emperor penguin mothers leave their eggs with the dads for months to get food and know to come right when the baby will be born down to the exact day. And then, even though through their eyes all the penguins look the same, they know out of thousands which one is the male and her baby. Or the way our moms or best friends know when something is wrong even from miles away. It's kind of like magic, really. Our beings sometimes know things as if it's an uploaded piece of information that on the surface seems illogical, and maybe impossible, to have any rationale or proof that that knowing is indeed true. Especially if it can't be seen. Like love, or penguin-connection, or electricity; we can't always *see* it. With faith, like most of the powerful things we can't see in life that are evidently there, we instead feel it.

The Bible tells us that God sent us the Holy Spirit to live with us in our time on earth and teaches us how to truly know and follow God, gives us special gifts, is our helper and comforter, and guides us to truth (see John 14:16-17 and John 16:13). The Holy Spirit is what allows us to have supernatural guidance from God, rather than depending on our own human reasoning or rationale. What I knew was that I was not sick- I was called.

When it comes to the definition of accepting, believing and recognizing what is valid, the "above perspective" and my *belief* was that this was not something I *had*, this was something I was *going through*. I believed God was using my body as a vessel for a purpose. The diagnosis was such a small, tiny puzzle piece when looking at the larger picture. I never used the words "I have," because it wasn't my prognosis- only the diagnosis. I wasn't going to give life to the cancer. I was going to fiercely feed my ability to have faith in the truth the Holy Spirit was guiding me to: "You are going to be ok. You are a vessel. This has a purpose. I understand you hear what you are hearing, but I need you to trust me."

Mikey and I were talking one day and he naturally was using the word, "cancer". I hated saying that word. I was staring out the window and I confidently said,

"We're not going to continuously use that word. I'm not giving life to it. From now on, it's the C-word."

<u>Riding Shotgun</u>

Everything started to happen so fast. When I first got diagnosed, I was both strong and fragile. I didn't want to be left alone because I was terrified to be in my thoughts at first. The thing that intimidated me the most was the thought of getting to a place where my fear overpowered my faith, I would become chaos and spiral into darkness. I didn't want to move into that space at all costs. I was so afraid of drowning in darkness that I immediately went into power mode *ON* to make sure I didn't go there. I did everything I could to avoid that specifically. In hindsight, it was shear survival mode. My survival mode was a lot stronger than I thought in some amazing ways and some not so much. And, really looking in depth, parts of my strong survival mode came from my childhood and growing up, while many good and productive parts came from my years of personal development and the faith in the Lord I found as an adult.

During the first week or so after finding out the results, Mikey could see I was afraid to be alone and he asked me if I wanted to come out with him in the day while working. I was like a lost innocent child during that time. So, for a couple weeks, I went out on jobs with him cleaning gutters. I was up on the roofs and did the dirty work. I didn't care what I had to do, I just didn't want to leave his side. He graciously allowed me to have shotgun and tag along like the best friends we are. Not that I was great or the most efficient at the jobs. Sometimes I was even more of a hassle I'm sure. But, I came and I worked hard and had my mind occupied. We'd smile and just go through the day together. It was peaceful up on the roofs. In hindsight, it's one of my sweetest memories I have of him and our marriage.

On the first day up on the roof I got a call from my assigned nurse. She started talking to me about what the trajectory was going to look like: She was assigned to be my support, schedule my appointments, check in with me, connect me with doctors, and guide me through the process. All I remember was that one of my very first questions was asking whether I was going to need to do chemo or not. I really didn't want to do chemo. She gave me long answers that it was all going to depend on what the doctors felt would be necessary and what the journey would lead us to.

CHAPTER 5

<u>The Hunger Games</u>

My adventure in the wilderness began. It was like I got dropped off in a *Hunger Games* type of situation where I knew my assignment and my only choice was to move forward or die for lack of more compassionate words; obstacle to obstacle, test after test. My imagination was seeing each spiritual test, mental push, doctor's appointment or test result as a new summons to contest in the dangerous yet adventurous wilderness. I was being tested, pruned, broken, shaped, molded and stretched, while moving closer to the spiritual perfection the bible talks about with every obstacle. Becoming savvy, dodging arrows and traps, and moving swiftly while on guard. We all know how Hunger Games went: you weren't able to leave until you were the last one standing. I knew I didn't have the option to just "leave" this wilderness. I was in it until completion. What motivated me to give my very best under that pressure is what we learn in James in the Bible: ***"Consider it a sheer gift, friends, when tests and challenges come at you from all sides. You know that under pressure, your faith-life is forced into the open and shows its true colors. So don't try to get out of anything prematurely. Let it do its work so you become mature and well developed, not deficient in any way" (James 1:2-4).*** If we keep going we will lack nothing. I was being trained. Up next in my journey was an MRI.

CHAPTER 6

It was the same hospital we had been coming to, but this was an unfamiliar floor and area we hadn't been to. I was hopeful, smiling, and had a pep in my step. Even when I started to feel a little fear, I'd smile. I'd intentionally be joyful to anyone I encountered and learned throughout the years to be expectant of good, to walk and talk it, and to "fake it 'till ya make it." If I wasn't going to have a choice in walking through this, I was going to do it with joy. This was my first experience at hospital staff starting to treat me "differently" if you will. I think once people find out that you have the C-word, their demeanor can change. I had to learn that I had to be extremely patient and graceful with this. However, whenever people would treat me differently it chipped away at my hope and I'd buck up and turn it into a humble challenge to choose joy and exemplify it. There are certain looks and tones you get. For me, it made me feel like I was destitute for bad. It always made things seem somber; they felt bad for me when I knew the battle was already won, so my frequency didn't match. I heavily leaned on the Holy Spirit to remind me of the truth and for comfort in my boldness.

I was nervous about the MRI but they told me Mikey could come in. They injected me with stuff to make the C-word glow, (*how weird is science by the way?*), I put on the gown and they gave me these headphones that were supposed to play "soothing spa music." I still laugh a little when I think of that because you honestly couldn't hear the music at all. I didn't realize why they were even giving me headphones but I was about to find out.

They explained to me what the scan was going to show them, to make sure the C-word wasn't anywhere else, and to get a more comprehensive look. I just kept taking deep breaths. The machine was huge and I was to lay face down and be overly emphasized, incredibly still for what seemed like an eternity. The tech warned me that the machine was going to be extremely loud, and it was. I quickly figured out why they gave me some headphones!

When I was laying down the tech told me that Mikey was going to be able to sit facing me in a chair. There were mirrors in the machine so that even though I was face down, the way they were positioned, I'd be able to see him but wouldn't be able to hear him. Mikey responded to the tech, "Oh, that's ok, we won't be talking. I am here for support. She's going to be talking to God the whole time." Mikey looked at me, nodded with a closed mouth smile, I gave him a gentle smile back and then we both looked at the tech. There was a pause with the tech staring at us in humble wonderment, and he said, "you ready?"

The deafening noise started. Mikey and I were just staring in each others' eyes; I saw such a softness in his eyes that was worried. I was tearing up in frustration and fear that I was there in the first place and what I was there for. My eyes blinked and the tears came out while trying to be as still as I possibly could for the machine. I never lost my gaze on him in the mirror and Mikey mouthed to me, "I love you." He couldn't see my mouth moved back but I whispered, "I love you too."

God, Come Down Now

I closed my eyes and I started to talk to God. When I do this sometimes, I enter a different realm. I left that machine. Life was happening in that room, but I had left to a different place. I was talking to God, calmly at first, and reciting some scripture I knew by heart. But I noticed that as I started to get more vulnerable and raw sitting and talking to God, it turned into an earnest, spiritual cry. I started praying on Psalms 18 and 23, which progressed with me desperately yelling for God to intervene. There was righteous anger in my spirit. I stood up, in the different place I was in. I wanted answers, ease from my fear and resolve. I just remember saying over and over what was screaming in my head, "God COME DOWN." I pictured me pointing down at myself in the machine and my husband in the chair. "Not next week, not tomorrow, not later, you come down RIGHT NOW. RIGHT NOW!" I continued.

Here's something I want you to know. Wherever you are, whatever you're going through, God knows your heart. You can't hide parts of you from God; not like we can in this world towards others and even ourselves.

He knows exactly where you are, what you're thinking before you even think it, before you can even think to formulate it into a "nice and neat" prayer, and He understands and feels your pain, anguish and fear.

The other thing I want you to know is something I didn't know before my walk with God. It's important. Maybe you don't know God as much as you would like, or at all for that matter. Maybe you've never wanted to know God and you picked up this book to just hear a healing story. Maybe, you don't know any Bible verses and you don't understand the Bible at all yet. Maybe you aren't consistent in going to church or are terrified to step foot in one because you think you're going to be zapped to the crisp by putting one toe on the pavement. Maybe you've been hurt by someone who was professing their faith or pushed religion versus faith in you. You think you're too damaged, filthy, sinned, problematic, lost, and far too gone for God to heal you, let alone hear you. I'm interceding on your behalf right now that this is a lie from the pit of hell. I can feel hell shake at me declaring this to you as I write it.

Even when you think you don't know Him, or if He hears you, or cares, or would help you in your crises now, He knows you. And He knows where you are. He knew you before you were a thought. He knit you from dust, with pure joy in His heart and magic in His hands in your mother's womb because He had plans for you. Love, for just you; reckless, unwavering, gut-wrenching, unconditional love, for you.

He hears you when you feel like He doesn't. He's there every moment even when you don't see Him. On another level deeper, He feels your pain and every emotion in real-time. He experienced every emotion and pain you can feel and understands. And on a level even deeper than that, you can talk to Him like you would talk to a friend, your mom, or your spouse. And if you don't have any of those, He wants to be all those things for you. Because He knows your every thought and feeling before you can even recognize or formulate it, He already knows what those things are, what you need and says, "It's ok. Come and talk to me about it." Raw, unfiltered, and pure.

So, there I was. Yelling in my spirit for the God of the Universe to come down at my command. It makes me laugh because I'm petite stature and I can just see God sitting on the bench I was imagining in the different realm where we were talking, leaning with one arm on the back of it, legs crossed, smiling and shaking his head as a parent does, while I'm just pacing back and forth completely freaking out. He was watching my adorable "authority" in action. The thing that I find so sweet about this is that even in my tantrum moment,

God knew my heart was pure. Pure and afraid, and even though He knew He fully had the authority, He was gracious with my feelings. He heard me in my distress, and He came down (Psalms 18). The atrociously loud noise stopped from the machine, my eyes opened and I was back in the room.

The guy told me to come out of the machine and the techs were in a room doing the scans; there was glass they could see through to where we were. They came outside of the room and something felt off. They all had looks on their faces that were trying to keep it cool without being obvious. The tech said to me that my doctor of all doctors, coincidentally passed through the room while I was doing the MRI and happened to take a peek at the scans while they were coming through. They wanted me to head upstairs back to the same breast center I had been to before because they wanted to do another ultrasound right then. Something was wrong.

"Is something wrong? Why would they want me to come upstairs after looking at the scan unless something is bad?" I asked. He didn't have a straight answer and said they just wanted to look at a few things. And, they *happened* to have a same day cancellation that was right at the end of this appointment. Sound familiar? Here was that coincidental irony again. What was supposed to only be one appointment ended up being hours and a few appointments.

We walked upstairs and they took me into the exact same breast center. This place was extremely familiar to me at this point. They had me undress on top and explained that they wanted to get another ultrasound based on what they saw:

First unannounced appointment of the day. Still no answers and panic started overwhelming me. After the ultrasound, they said they now wanted a mammogram so that they had all the possible angles, measurements, and imagery they could get to really see what we were dealing with: Second unannounced appointment of the day. Because of my age, and more so because this whole journey they expected that this wasn't the C-word, everything was done backwards. Normally, they would do a mammogram as preventative first, then an ultrasound, then the MRI. They don't like to do mammograms on women under the age of 40, preferably 50. Why? Because it's dangerous for us and can *cause* the C-word. Are you as confused as me in 2019? Anyways, I get into the mammogram room and the nurse had the "sorry" tone and eyes. At this point, I felt defeated and afraid. I was physically and emotionally tired from being there that long unannounced and without any answers as to why yet. She said she would be right back and I just started to cry.

"I've Got God"

I was overwhelmed for the first time that day. It felt like when you're at that point in your training that you actually feel like you don't want to push anymore. She came back in and asked if I was okay. I wiped my tears and I stood up and nodded. I took a deep breath, rolled my shoulders back and we made our way to the machine. She looked at me, gave me a sweet sympathetic closed smile, gave a quick rub on my back and said, "Let's do this." I always wore my cross necklace my husband gave me on my neck. Thinking back, I never took that cross off my neck. I wore it for comfort and protection, but also for people in the doctor's office to know who was with me. It was a way of talking about God without even talking about Him sometimes. I wanted to bring Him everywhere, talk about Him every chance I got, and open a window as to why I had supernatural faith. Part of my mission in having the C-word was having the chance to bring Him into a world that is so matter of fact, based on numbers, results and science. It's a place where you're not supposed to see things you can't explain. It was my privilege to talk about Him, and since people feel bad for you when you have the C-word, they'd listen. They got a chance to feel Him without anything being shoved down their throat. With genuine light in my heart, I shamelessly took advantage of that. So, with my cross on my neck, she told me that we would need to move it to do the scan and asked if that was okay. She helped me spin it around so that it was hanging down my back.

When getting one of the side images, she asked me what the tattoo on my left rib cage said. "Find your bliss," I quietly replied. She tenderly looked at me, with the most disheartened eyes and tone, and said, "It must be really hard for you to do that right now." I looked her square in her eyes, with gentle eyes and a huge light-hearted smile and said, "No, I've got God." I remember still smiling and looking down and I could feel her looking at me with perplexity and gentle shock. She stepped back behind the wall to get the image. It was moments like this that God was giving me what we call grace. Supernatural calm and joy in pure chaos.

I began to notice something about my peace and joy in my circumstance. The more positive, joyous, and calm I was, the more people saw God without me needing to talk about Him. There was no religious talk, forced conversation or unwillingness to be open. It was two humans sharing an empathetic moment. Relentless faith was exemplified through me because of my choice and God's grace and ability He was giving me because of that choice. People were often confused, puzzled and shocked that I wasn't overly anxious, generally didn't have any outward fear, was happy, sure, calm, and even joyous. Jesus was the only explanation I truthfully have for this, but I willingly made myself a vessel to display it. Catch that?

The Size Of The Battle

She told me to hang tight so that the doctor could look over everything. She came back into the room and said they wanted another ultrasound. *ANOTHER* ultrasound: Third unannounced appointment. Mikey and I sat in this small waiting room within the breast center. We started to get anxious and restless wanting answers. Mikey was angry at this point. We sat in the room and I remember he started to move into hard charging mode; the profanity and impatience was understandably coming out. He was scared. He started to demand answers and they had better do it quickly. I'll never forget him slamming both hands on the table when talking to the nurse. It was like I was watching a scene and I wasn't in the room. They understood they needed to move and move quick.

Mikey has that way about him. His presence is powerful. He was angry and trying to protect his wife, and I was also angry, watching my husband suffer because of what was happening. It pained me. I wished I could have held him, and not in the physical sense. How do you hold someone when the thing they are panicking about is you? They now had us both in the back room and after quickly doing the ultrasound they had me sit up and turned the lights on. The radiologist and two nurses were in the room and they finally brought us into the light on what the heck was going on.

They took a deep breath and the tension in the room was high. Very high. The radiologist in a quiet but stern voice looked at us and told us that when she looked at the MRI that morning, "coincidentally" walking by, they saw that what they originally thought was a tumor measuring anywhere from maybe 1-2cm, was actually about a little over 5cm. There was bone-chilling panic in the room. My face went white. My heart started to race. And I remember I couldn't even look at Mikey because I could feel the panic in him even though he had a calm demeanor. I stared straight ahead. Mikey immediately jumped in but it was as if all the sound started to phase out like background noise. He stood up and started demanding the next appointment. He aggressively demanded in a very boisterous voice, "Well, can't you just take it out?! When is the next surgery? Who do we need to talk to?" He was clapping his hands how people do when they say "*let's get the show on the road.*"

Everyone in the breast center could hear us I'm sure. The tears started to fall down my steel face. They were going back and forth but there was a loud ringing in my ears. She was intimidated and was trying to get Mikey to calm down, explaining it's not that simple. Mikey demanded that it was. You can start to see where I get my, "don't take no for an answer" optimism. I looked at Mikey and told him it was okay. I felt for him. And I appreciated him. I respected him. We both wanted resolve. I calmly asked the doctor what was next. She said they needed to do another biopsy. "Well let's do it right now," Mikey said. "This is where you guys did it last time so I know you can do it now." The doctor said they wouldn't be able to do it that same day; they had other patients that were scheduled, and even if they wanted to do it which they of course did, they need a specific medication to inject in the breast to numb it that isn't held in that same building and they would need it transferred over. They said they probably could get us in for an appointment in two to three weeks.

Mikey wasn't going to stop. He demanded that they make something happen that day. I didn't have any urge to stop him or calm him down. The doctor felt Mikey's pain; I knew she did. The nurses felt his pain. We all did. Everyone was looking at me sitting on the table, speechless. I was trying to pray to keep myself calm. I was frozen. She told him she understood that this was incredibly difficult for him, for us and even for them. She sighed, and told the nurse to look at the schedule. The nurse nodded and left. I closed my eyes and was just asking God to come, to please help, and telling Him that I was scared.

The nurse came back into the room. She quietly and in disbelief told the radiologist that the next person had cancelled. *Another cancellation*. My eyes lifted, Mikey perked up, the doctor was in perplexed disbelief. She looked at me and quickly said to the nurse, "Call the other building to get the medication transferred." The mission was on. The nurse excitedly smiled big and quickly went to her assignment. We did the second biopsy that day; The fourth unannounced appointment. That day, because of the insane, unexplainable, "ironic," "coincidental," series of multiple events, we speeded up my C-word process by about a month. God heard me in my fiery, desperate, child-like outcry in the MRI. And, as I asked Him to, because He is good like that, He did come down. We were watching God in real-time. I was in complete, speechless awe. We all were. God hears you, He is moving on your behalf, and with a servant heart and some faith, He will show you that even by the hour and minute, He can move in miraculous ways.

CHAPTER 7

I want to cover something before we move on in the story. We access God's miracles because we have faith. This is required and what God is looking for.

He isn't expecting us to never have fear; He is calling us to give it to Him and expecting us to know that He is bigger than the fear.

He is bigger than the circumstance. And when we do this, He graciously bit by bit, will show us just enough for us to know it was Him. Eventually, these bit by bit moments string together and turn into our major miracles. This was my second considerable observation that God doesn't know time like we do. He works miracles that are so great and so beyond, and they can happen in a moment's time. He has the supernatural ability to move, shape and shift on His command. His orchestration is divine and with expectant faith, He wants to show you what He can do that no one else can. This is the magic.

A Grace Capsule

At this point, the only people who knew were still Michael and my best friend. My mom was living with Michael and I at the time and I never told her until about two weeks after I found out. Mikey kept pushing me to tell her and I'd just keep arguing not yet or that I wasn't ready. In hindsight, I think it was on purpose that she was still with us at that time while I went through this. Even though it was rough on Michael and I at times to have her living with us, not because we didn't enjoy her being around or love her of course, but everything happens for a reason. It was without a doubt comforting to have my mom with me in this process and have her help when the time came.

She was under the same roof as us and had no clue what I had been going through and that her only daughter had just got diagnosed with the C-word. Telling my mom was extremely difficult because I knew it was going to crush her. It would crush any mother. Even though when I was younger our relationship wasn't the best, we began to grow with God's grace. She loved me tremendously and more than anything and I knew it. I knew she was going to panic. I knew she was going to completely freak out and lose it.

I was working extremely hard to protect my mental and spiritual space that I thought, when I tell her she's going to completely lose it and it's going to make me lose it. I also was not prepared to see my mom in pain. I didn't want her to be afraid even though I did need her. I didn't want her to be rid

51

with worry. I wanted to protect her like I did my husband. I wanted to protect myself. Each time someone new found out, it felt like hearing it for the first time and going through the shock all over again in the beginning. One morning, it was finally time to tell her. Mikey looked at me and he said, "Airam, you need to tell her" in a stern voice. I was fiddling around with something in our room but I heard him loud and clear, and I knew I needed to. I walked into her room and Mikey stood in the doorway. I came by her bedside and I told her that I needed to tell her something. "Just promise me that you're not going to freak out. Promise?" She sat up and she was worried. "Just tell me anak, you're starting to make me scared. What's wrong, you can tell me." Anak means child in Tagalog; She's called me that since I was a baby.

I couldn't spit it out. I had told her earlier I was going to the doctor because I felt a lump in my boob but she assured me that it was no problem, she's had lumps before and it will be benign. It was such a casual conversation; she never thought twice, like I didn't, that it could be anything to really worry about. The C-word would never even be a possibility. "Remember how I told you I went to the doctors a few weeks ago to get a check up for the lump I was feeling?" I asked. She had a puzzled look on her face and confidently said, "Well yea?" I still couldn't get it out, and she just said, "Airam...what? Come on you can tell me." She was getting anxious and I finally just said it. "I went to the doctors and have been getting some tests done. They said the lump is cancer."

There was a long pause and she was confused. "It's cancer? Are they sure?" I nodded and said,"yep." She immediately asked if she could hug me. She pulled the blankets back and sat up in her bed on her knees, and we hugged. My spirit felt peace not just within me, but within her. Now, I was confused. In my survival mode, I interjected, "I don't know how to fully explain it, but I know everything is going to be fine!" I was preparing myself and getting a jump start before the hysterical crying, the freak out, and the bomb would go off in her.

She sat back in the bed, and to my complete shock, I noticed she was completely, miraculously, peculiarly calm. She looked at me and even she shook her head in disbelief of what she was saying and feeling. She said, "I don't know how to explain this but I feel completely peaceful. And you know me... I freak out about things. I don't know... I feel completely calm. My spirit is calm. I don't believe you found it how you did and when you did for God to not take you through it. You're going to be okay."

Mikey and I looked at each other in complete disbelief. This was what my pastor calls a "grace capsule." God will deliver us these capsules at special times, through things or people, to let you know He's with you. It's a divine message. It's an important reminder. This was a supernatural grace capsule that all three of us completely could not explain. God gave her a distinct calm that we knew was out of character and supernatural. It was a sweet rainbow moment God gave me as a sign of confirmation like He states in Genesis 9:12. We saw

God in real time again. I teared with an embrace of goodness and faith. A piece of Shalom.

Peace Amidst War

Let's quickly talk about peace. When I look up the word "peace" and pull up the dictionary definition that pops up on Google, what comes up is, "freedom from disturbance; tranquility" and "a state or period in which there is no war or a war has ended." I one thousand and fifty percent challenge this to a complete duel. The real words that came to my mind were "horse" and a derogatory word that follows that starts with the letter S. I, like Peter in the Bible, can have a bit of a sailors mouth but hey I'm a work in progress. I used to think of peace as the absence of war, because we all think of peace signs and hippies; "make peace not war." Or, I used to think of zen gardens, tranquil running water spa music, those patterns in the sand and doing yoga. Now, not that these things are not of peace; I'm exceptionally for meditation and I'll later walk you through how important this was in my healing, and am obviously for ending world war. But, the peace that Jesus is teaching us and is willingly offering is completely different. It is not, and I need to emphasize this, it is absolutely not the absence of war or the freedom from disturbance. It is not the promise and absence of "bad."

It is not the promise or absence of life happening, hard learning lessons, pain, heartbreak, betrayal, storms or tests. In fact, I dare to say something I wanted to be in denial about for a long time when I first started my faith walk five years ago. I heard it said that often times, when we decide to follow God and furthermore live to share Him, we become a voluntary soldier in a much larger battle. Did you hear that? A much larger *battle*; a war. And you are fighting in it. Far from the absence of war. What this means is that you have now become a threat to power and authority of darkness. And with that, arrows and attack will come your way. In coming other books, I'll go into this with far more depth. But right now, I want you to know that Jesus' peace does not mean the absence of bad. You have to understand this to understand His goodness.

Sometimes people will say, "They love God and they're devoted Christians. Why would God do that to them if He was good?" God did not send the C-word to you. He didn't give the C-word to me. However, He *allowed* this to happen in order for His glory to be shown. And He wants it to be shown! You are stronger than you know and perfectly equipped because He is in you. And the good news, is that God always wins because it is written. Hang on with everything you have to this. He is good. He is for your good. He wins. And good wins.

So, when going through this and people would look at me and be utterly shocked that I was filled with peace, expectant faith, love, hope and genuine unexplainable joy, it did not mean that I wasn't experiencing bad. It didn't mean there was an absence of the valley I was walking in. That as a human, I wasn't going through shattering moments of pain, fear and every emotion in between. No. What it meant was that God was supernaturally carrying me to deliver what He promises for those who love Him; GOOD!

He is the Prince of Peace and can, will, and wants to fill you and embrace you with such superhuman peace in the midst of pure chaos; where you are expected to otherwise be in sheer agony by standards of this world. He is there to help you go inward and work through your own setbacks, negative beliefs, hurt, fears and flaws. I've witnessed it. It's real. And every bit of it I knew was not me, and I never took credit for it. I still won't. Open your heart to experiencing this; it's going to take practice. But it is your right, and He wants this for you.

CHAPTER 8

Continuing my voyage through the wilderness, next up we met with the surgeon I got paired with who was going to be doing the C-word removal. He was older, you could tell had been a doctor for many years, had white hair and was so casual in a way that it made you feel as if you were a number. I went into every appointment with joyful positivity and a naturally high frequency that was very unnatural for the circumstance and place. I was aware of that. This guy, did not match that at all. He was short and to the point, matter of fact, casual in delivery with heavy information and inauthentically smiled a lot. He was cold to me and our energies collided immediately. I'm big on energy. I can sense things on extremely deep levels without needing to know or see much and more often than not, my empath intuition never steered me wrong. My radar was going off with this guy. It was like all of this was nothing and "*sure, I'll do the surgery*," was the overall theme. When talking about what his plan of action was for me and what he thought would be my treatment plan, he bluntly and casually answered while writing the chart notes from the appointment.

I strongly dislike when people don't make eye contact with me when talking.

"Either chemo or radiation before to shrink it, then double mastectomy, chemo and radiation after, then hormone therapy for years proceeding. You're also going to want to get the genetic testing done because if this is genetic, we'll need to take out your uterus since it dramatically ups your chances of you getting uterine cancer." He clicked the pen and looked up, took a deep breathe and then gave me a rehearsed spiel about how this was a difficult journey and he understood, but that I was in good hands.

He gave me a few dates he had available to do the surgery like they were coffee dates and told me to think about it and get back to him. Total blank stares, and even though my jaw wasn't physically dropped, it felt like it was. I wanted to cry. There was a huge lump in my throat and I felt like I had got punched in the stomach. From the casual and insistent demand as a professional that this was my only course, to me possibly not having children, all in a matter of 20 minutes was appalling and felt disgusting really.

He gave Michael and I firm hand shakes and said it was nice to meet us. I looked at Mikey and I knew in my spirit none of this sounded right. None of it felt right. This was not at all in the plan that God put in my spirit; not that God gave me an exact plan or layout by any means, but this was not in it. I had a knowing that I truly don't know how to explain, like most of my knowings. He came back inside to give the print out review of the appointment and he walked to the nurse station and left us to leave on our own. We started to walk down the hallway, I paused in my tracks and looked down at the paper and Mikey asked what was wrong. I told him that I just wanted to ask the doctor a question.

I turned around and walked back to the nurses station and didn't care if I was or wasn't supposed to go there. I interrupted what he was doing and said, "Excuse me I just have a question." "Is this the only option, the *only* course of action that you're telling me is possible? I have to do chemo? And a double mastectomy?" He looked at me and said, "Well, a lot of that part depends on your oncologist. I'm the surgeon. But based on my expertise and knowledge, yes, this is what I suggest and more than likely what they will tell you as well." He was prideful in his answer.

I thanked him and started walking towards Mikey with determination in my step. I had the confirmation I needed. I shoved the paper in my purse and told Mikey that wasn't my doctor as I passed him. Mikey caught up to me, put his arm around my shoulder and said, "okay." He laughed and said, "I didn't think so." Onto the next. Cue some Jay Z. I'm spiritual but you know, I'm a little thug.

Pieces To Your Promise

I'd say that one of the hardest parts of this journey for me was when it was on the table, by their periscope, that I might not be able to have children, and that if I were able to have them, that that would be, or shouldn't be, for a very long time.

Writing this makes me relive the devastation and heartbreak that was in my stomach at the thought, and it still makes the lump come back in my throat and tears well in my eyes. Being passed it now, I wish I could give myself a hug in those moments. Mikey and I had only been married for a year and a half. This aspect of the journey brought a lot of stretching and a deeper sense of faith and fight in me. It also brought a deeper, interesting understanding of the Lord's perfect orchestration.

I have always dreamed about being a mother. Part of me knows that when my time comes, it's going to wash over me a whole different realm of supernatural purpose. It's always been one of the greatest things I've looked forward to, one of the things I know in every fiber I was designed to do when the time is right. I have a deep understanding that it will be one of the biggest, most important duties I will have; it is my truest belief looking in hindsight and going through other trials recently, that my children will be some of the mightiest to the Kingdom. And, with that brings warfare. I'm proud to be a threat to darkness. And I'm proud to know my children will be ones fiercely fighting to defeat it as well. To be Kingdom Kids who grow to change and impact the world in positive ways.

Mikey and I always wanted to be parents throughout our relationship and we planned on getting pregnant the year I got diagnosed. We were planning on going on some trips earlier in the year then coming home to try and conceive. Our plans were derailed, and now they were being threatened entirely. This was the first moment I was tempted to yell, "*This is not fair.*" I imagined me yelling to the sky in darkness with rain and thunder and the wind howling. I felt as though I wanted to hit that boxing bag; not with good training form but with anguish and anger. But, I immediately took the thought captive.

Declare, Baby. Declare.

I stayed focused best I could. This was the first part of the journey that I started to understand the power of declaration. On Easter that year, we went over to friends' house for dinner. I remember the guys were talking, being guys, and it was just the girls around the dinner table. They knew about the C-word by now. One of the ladies mentioned that she had just read the book, "Outwitting the Devil" by Napoleon Hill. This is an incredible read by the way. We were talking about the book and she casually mentioned the notion that the enemy understands how we pray; he understands that we have the power to declare versus beg God. I stopped her and asked her to repeat what she had said. I don't think she even recognized the importance of what she just said for me. My body instantly and curiously perked up and it was like my spirit had unlocked the next level in an adventurous video game. The notion that the book explains is that the enemy knows that we actually have the power to ask God of what we want in expectation, and that if it is in His will, He will do it. He knows that this key is in fact in the bible repetitively, but we don't seem to understand it to it's full effect. So, we beg and repeatedly ask in what I now think of as lack of expectation, faith, and sureness instead of declare unwaveringly the things God promises you in His word. Two of the verses that immediately came to my mind were Proverbs 18:21 Death and life are in the power of the tongue: and they that love it shall eat the fruit thereof, and James 1:6 But when you ask, you must believe and not doubt, because the one who doubts is like a wave of the sea, blown and tossed by the wind.

Proverbs is teaching us to be careful of what we say which derives from what we think because both life and death can come from how powerful these are. Those that understand this have the power to reap good fruit and those that are loose with words or thoughts will likewise see a different outcome. James is teaching us that furthermore, when you ask, you cannot waiver and have doubt. You ask fully in, all the way, and expectantly. Otherwise you and your prayers are "tossed by the wind;" loose and without a steak in the ground. I simultaneously was reading the book "The Secret" by Rhonda Byrne. This book powerfully explains the simple rule of the law of attraction: what you think and feel determine what you attract in your life. When you are exercising this, it is essential that you focus on the positives not the negatives. In other words, it is crucial to focus on what you do want and not the things that you don't want. For example, changing "I really don't want to fail the quiz" to "I'm excited to get my test results back that I passed." It clicked, and this changed everything for me.

I started to apply this to every thought, every desired outcome, every detail of what the journey was going to look like down to the appointments, and down to what was happening within my body. This obviously takes practice, but I was quick to move into action. However, getting the genetic testing done was the first benchmark where I believe we saw this come into play. I declared every day that it wasn't genetic. There was a lot riding on this; Not only the fact of possibly taking my uterus out but the course of my treatment plan. If it was genetic, chemo was going to need to happen. I'd say, "My body will show God's miracle of being completely cancer free. This cancer will be gone forever and by your grace and miracle, Michael and I will be able to conceive beautiful, healthy children after the next two years." Over and over and over and over again. This was my biggest, boldest prayer.

I worked backwards in my mind and interestingly enough, looking back, the main thing that was the benchmark for my healing in my mind was our children. If I were C-word free and I had children in the next few years, that would mean everything in the interim went in our favor; including the genetic testing, no chemo and being cancer free. We started to recruit a few people here and there to pray at the church as well at that time. It came time to go to the appointment and the lady was so incredibly somber. I'll never forget it.

She naturally had a very quiet, meek, gentle nature but she was talking to us so incredibly slow, trying to explain every detail and rationale behind everything, and talking about all the negative outcomes that would come if this were genetic and that that was why they wanted to test for it. She left the room for a minute and Mikey and I were upset. We went in there optimistic, energy high, joyful and she brought us down in an instant. Again, I truthfully don't believe this was her or any medical professional's intention to do this. I really believe they're doing the best they can with something difficult, they're probably not used to oddly upbeat people, and have no idea what's going to best serve an individual at a fragile time; at least most of them.

When she came in, we didn't plan on this but it ended up just coming out, maybe at wits end of frustration with the situation, that we really did not like the verbiage she was using and it felt like the whole conversation we just had was negative. I remember us asking her if there was any positive and staring at her blankly. She wasn't a bad person at all. But I think it was an important lesson to bring something to the table. We were filled with light in an otherwise dark place. A lot of people couldn't understand it, and we learned to graciously change the vibration around us to match what we believed. You're allowed to do this gracefully and with kindness at the root. Her demeanor started to change and I honestly knew she was on our side; she was sorry and did want the same results as us.

Mental Rehearsal

From before we went in to get the testing to when we were going to get the results, I intensely practiced the law of attraction and praying with declaration. I began to even envision and rehearse mentally what it was going to look and sound like when I'd get the call that it wasn't genetic. What it was going to feel like. I rehearsed the joy and excitement in my heart.

The day came that I got the call. I had just pulled up to the gym and was sitting in my car when I got a local number that was unfamiliar ringing in. I picked it up anxious if it was going to be the results, and it was. It was actually the same tech that we met with for the genetic testing. I remember there was a tiny pause of fear, I snapped into position and said to myself, "This is it!" My heart rushed and she said, "I have some really good news for you!" She was smiling from ear to ear from the other side of the phone and she had pure joy in her spirit. I knew in that split moment she really was for us and it was like we had a non verbal exchange of apology and forgiveness. I could feel through the phone she was genuinely relieved and celebrating with me.

"Airam, the testing came back negative. The cancer is not genetic!" I had her on speaker and I literally screamed out loud in joy at the top of my lungs. My butt was hopping up and down in the seat and my left hand made a jackpot motion while I closed my eyes and yelled, "Thank you Lord!" She said, "I'm so happy for you, have a great rest of your day ok?" I celebrated in the car for a quick minute and then I welled up with tears of joy and got one more shout in. It felt and went exactly how I imagined it would and my gratitude and relief rushed through me. Sometimes when God answers a prayer, especially in real time, the Holy Spirit can overwhelm you with an indescribable joy. I was silent for a moment and gave God praise. He was going to do it, in all His righteousness, mercy and goodness. It's what I believed. I skipped into the gym that day, *literally*, and high-fived the front desk person. We had been regulars at our gym, knew almost everyone in there, and came in nearly every day. Because we only told a few people that I was going through the C-word, no one in there knew the silent battle I had been fighting. They just saw me getting in really great shape not knowing my motivation was a lot more intense than they'd probably imagine. There were many days I'd run on my specific treadmill for miles and cry while my fear, anger and frustration were being let out. I always chose that treadmill because directly in line-eye's view, there was a sign that said, "You have what it takes." I'd stare at it without blinking and it would feel like I was floating while running miles and miles. It was just me, God, and those words. That day, I was crying tears of joy.

CHAPTER 9

I was reading the Book of Mark in the bible this morning about when Jesus was confronted in a panic by a man begging for His help; his young daughter was right at death's door about to die. Also, there's a woman in the same crowd with a blood sickness (Mark 5:21-43). The woman who was constantly bleeding for twelve years tried everything she possible could and nothing worked. While Jesus was making His way to the little girl through the large gathering crowd, she took a bold risk to simply reach for Jesus' robe in passing because she believed that by just touching His garment she would be healed. It further tells us that Jesus literally had to try and figure out who touched His robe, but once He does, He says to her in Mark 5:34: "Your faith has made you well. Go in peace. Your suffering is over." Notice how He says to her, "your faith." He doesn't say her touching His robe or Him physically performing a healing ritual. He knew His healing power had been used on someone by the simple passing touch of His garment but he didn't even know who it was. It was her boldness and faith that activated His power towards her. Let's keep going.

Then, as Jesus is still talking to this woman, Jairus receives the message that his daughter is now dead. I can imagine his anguish in this moment. A father desperately trying to save his daughter knowing Jesus is their only hope probably lost all his hope in that split moment. Everyone around Jairus even told him, since she's already dead to not bother Jesus anymore. It was over. The sentence was made. But I love what comes next. Jesus simply overhears the others give the "news" to Jairus. No need to even try they said. There's no need to bother Jesus anymore, as if they would now become a burden. "Don't bother," are such devastatingly hopeless words.

How many times have others said this to you in your life about your dreams, marriage, health, joy, money, broken relationships, hopes or your relationship with God? How many times have you said this to yourself?

Talitha Koum

Jesus calmly says to Jairus, "Don't be afraid. Just have faith" (Mark 5:36). He says nothing more than that. Jesus then proceeds to make it to their mourning home. There was weeping, wailing in pain, neighbors gathering, and people talking about what happened. Jesus asks, "why the commotion?" After Jesus suggests the little girl is not dead but simply sleeping, everyone is laughing in sarcasm. He proceeds to go into the room where the young girl was, with just her parents and His disciples. He says two words while holding her lifeless hand: "Talitha koum" (Mark 5:41). The Bible tells us this means, "Little girl, get up." She immediately stands up and walks around. While her parents are in complete and almost frightened awe of this impossible miracle, Jesus then tells them to go get her some food to eat as if nothing happened.

In just the proceeding text, after He heals the young girl, it explains that Jesus left and went back to Nazareth which is His hometown. As He's teaching the people, everyone is mocking Him, refusing to believe in Him, and had an attitude towards Him like, "*Who does this guy think he is?*" Mark 6:5-6 says, "And because of their unbelief, He couldn't do any miracles among them except to place His hands on a few sick people and heal them. And He was amazed at their unbelief." What strikes me profusely is the sequence of events where just before this in another town, Jesus performs these two inconceivable miracles that the people of Nazareth don't know about, and He's not quick to try and explain to them what He did for them to believe. The next thing that stands out to me is it clearly says that because of their unbelief, He COULDN'T do anything miraculous before them. Nothing was activated. They gave Him the exact opposite of faith and took it a step further to mock. Does this mean that the power wasn't available? Does it mean that Jesus didn't have the ability to perform the miracles? That He wasn't capable? No. It means they didn't believe therefore they didn't see. *The faith needed to come before the evidence and before the miracles.*

We could wrap the whole book up with just that notion. Please, don't miss this.

I'm also struck by the fact that Jesus considers the smallest of His work to be laying hands on a few sick people and healing them, as if this is casually nothing to Him, because He's that great! This is the same way the woman with the blood sickness gets healed in simple passing! It's like when a great athlete breaks a world record or when Kobe Bryant put up an explosive 60 points during his final NBA game. They just look around confused like, *"What? This is what I do."*

Activate Your Miracles With Your Faith

If in the midst of their complete and utter disbelief, Jesus just so happens to *"oh by the way"* heal a few sick people, what does this say about what He can do for you? And what does this say you can activate with just even a little faith? What about with full faith and expectancy? I feel in my spirit that I'm talking to *someone* right now. You, little boy and you, little girl. I'm pointing you out in the crowd and saying, "Get up!" You are not done yet. I'm staring at just you and walking towards you. "It's time for YOU to get up and walk!" They may have given you the sentence, diagnosis or likely outcome. You may feel surrounded by people in your circumstance and they're saying, "There's no use troubling Jesus now." Your situation may feel and look impossible and dead. And believe me, I know what dead feels and looks like in situations. Everything around you may look completely opposite from what you believe. But my sweet friend, don't be afraid. Just have faith.

Jesus' power hasn't run out. Jesus' power isn't unavailable to you and He is able. If He did it then He is able to do the same now. You have to get up! It is time for you to activate your faith so that we can see the miracles in your circumstance. You are not alone. I'm standing on the ropes in your corner of the ring right now yelling to you that it's not over until God says it's over! It never is.

I'm staring at you lying with your face on the side of that mat, body motionless. Now is the time that you bend your shaky elbow and you put one glove on that mat. "Jesus is a healer." Put your weary weight on that truth and slowly lift your other glove and put it on that mat saying, "Jesus is *my* healer." Lift your upper body up on your knees. Feel the loud chaos around you. Feel the enemy afraid and put one foot on that mat *declaring*, "Jesus is a healer." Lift your head. Put that other foot on the mat and slowly get up. Get up!

You get up, off balance, one eye swollen shut, the other you can barely see out of and ears ringing. Stand in your belief. Believe!

You do this over, and over, and over, and over again. And although it's not pretty, this is what wins battles.

Although most of the time this will be in private with no applause, God sees you. And just when you feel like you truly can't get up any more, your miracle, whatever God says that is, will show up.

My friend, Jesus is your healer. He redeems. He delivers. Don't be afraid. Just have faith. Stand firm in the ring and get up as many times as you need to. The famous Rocky says, "It's not about how you can hit. It's about how hard you get hit and keep moving forward. It's about how much you can take. That's how winning is done."

Surrender your fear.

When we hear the word, surrender, many think of weakness. We want control in the situation. In the C-word world, and many other circumstances in our life, it can feel like we have zero control. And more often than not, we don't. In actuality, the hardest and most powerful thing you can do is surrender. Why? Because it is the most unnatural thing to us. Your power and faith are *in* surrender. It takes the most strength to surrender.

Surrendering to God's abilities and not yours, what He can do and not what the world says can be done. His promise is that He works only for your good in His timing and His way. Surrender to the process of winning without any shortcuts. There are no shortcuts here, friend! I know that surrendering your fear, standing up again and again and choosing faith thousands of times a day seems tedious, feels draining, rigorous, unseen and at times pointless. But I can assure you, it's not. There are no tap outs on this journey. It is *you* that needs to walk *through* this. You were chosen for this. You have everything it takes inside of you. I know that, He knows that, and it's time for you to know that. You have victory in every fiber of your being. What the victory looks like is up to Jesus, but it belongs to you.

CHAPTER 10

So far, I had gotten all green lights minus the unexpected size of the tumor. The C-word was, as of now, localized in only one breast, stage one and non-aggressive. It was the kind that would respond to hormone therapy, and it wasn't genetic. In meeting with my oncologist, he said, "Of any kind of cancer to have, especially with breast, this is the best kind to have." I remember thinking to myself how strange of a juxtaposition that was. Nonetheless, I was ecstatic and extremely grateful this was the case for obvious reasons. *I actually saw it as a confirmation that this was not something I "had" but something I was "going through" as a vessel for God.*

But, even with all the green lights and everything seeming to point towards a miracle-in-the-making, there was still a giant obstacle aside from the fact that the C-word was in my breast to begin with. It's kind of like being ahead in the Hunger Games; you've made it this far and you're a finalist with just a few more people to eliminate, but you're *still* in the freaking Hunger Games. The close-to-finale challenge was that even though I was getting all these green lights, which to me logically meant I didn't need all the bells and whistles of conventional treatment, the oncologist thought otherwise. And very adamantly. He still wanted me to go through every rigorous form of ammo they had in their arsenal to eradicate the C-word and make sure it wouldn't come back. *Every single one:* Chemotherapy before, a double mastectomy (remove both my breasts), chemotherapy after, radiation after that if the pathology from the surgery suggested it was needed, and then place me on hormone therapy for minimum of five to ten years, but for life was encouraged.

One major problem. My spirit inside was violently screaming, "*This is not God's plan for me!*" It was deafeningly loud inside of me. Remember how intimately important it was for me to become a mom? When doing chemo, there are so many complications on the body that it greatly impacts fertility. On the hormone therapy, you cannot get pregnant because it would cause incredibly major complications to the baby. They were talking five to ten years.

Puzzle Pieces On The Box

With either of these, they weren't fitting the puzzle of the picture on the box God gave me: total healing, living C-word free with my husband, fulfilling huge plans the Lord has for me, and healthy children as a family within the next few years. I was unwavering in my faith at what God could do. Relentless actually. Just even the possibility of what I knew He could do was my hope and I clung for dear life. I fought tooth and nail in that ring against every doubt that they were deeming factual, every fear, every statistic they gave me, and every thought contradictory to the promise I believed I was going to receive. I believed in the progression of the miracle God was unfolding.

What Champions Are Made Out Of

I needed to be desperately intentional about asking God to allow me to hear the doctors but to give me clear discernment in my spirit. I declared joy and an operating frequency of love in and around me at all times. I always heard champion stories about the need to constantly choose. Choosing to get up again, choosing not go give up, choosing not to back down, choosing to choose faith. We all know that those things are hard, otherwise they wouldn't be champions. However, living it was different.

It exposed the truth of why and how those people won. Ugly, ruthless, and painstaking grit; What happened behind closed doors and internally to get them there.

To hear and witness is different than to experience. It hurt. The stretching. The carrying of boulders. The drowning. The mental training.

I still cry thinking about how bad it hurt to push at times but I wasn't going to give in. Not to prove I was strong or had it all together, but to walk in faith for what I believed. I felt like I needed to lead for myself, my family, and everyone around me. I had an obligation for what I was called to, and if God was going to choose me for such a task, I was going to give everything I had to finish. And although God was giving me supernatural grace to do it, giving everything I had round after round when I was exhausted was hard. What I realized was that the battle was fully mental and even more, entirely spiritual.

I remember after my first oncology appointment I was eerily quiet in the car. I just cried silently to myself looking out the window while Mikey drove. This was one of the first major times I felt defeat. My assigned nurse called me and asked me how it went, and I shared with her how disappointed I was because I really did not believe that chemo was the route for me personally. In emphasis, I am being very clear that this was me, my body, and what I believed the Spirit was telling me for me. Every single person is different but I knew what I knew for me. And when I know something in my faith, I don't and won't back down. She said, "Well, were you just really not wanting to do chemo?" "No, I just don't feel like it's right for me. It doesn't feel like my plan."

The Temptation To Ask Why

I cried and I felt like a school-aged Airam. The woman tried to comfort me that she knew it wasn't ideal but if the doctor advises it's the best route then it's what I should do, and that it's standard. It was the first, and only, time in the whole journey I felt myself ask, "*Why, God?*"

Something snapped in me immediately and said, "Do not ask why. When this is all said and done and victory is yours, the why will be answered. Just focus."

This may sound a bit harsh, but I instinctively never allowed myself to ask why again. When I started to feel the temptation to ask, I'd shift to one word and one word only: Focus. I hold myself to a high standard mentally. Remember how I said that spiraling was my biggest fear? Without question, if I were to ask why, it would place me in the position of a victim rather than a victor. "Why me," I believe, leads to the rabbit hole and quick descent to pity, lack of control, lack of composure, fear, and ultimately, lack of faith.

I believe asking why, when going through difficult trials we may not understand, surrenders the situation and leaves it open to be vulnerable. It opens a doorway for the enemy to sneak in and either slowly or rapidly devour your spirit in your thoughts, tricking you into thinking that they are real. It leads you to question what God promised you, and leads you to question who's voice is speaking; God, you, or the enemy. Listen to me. You are a human. As am I. I am not so Godly where I have never had doubtful thoughts or confusion. But your strategy and obligation is to not stay there. We will never fully evade doubtful thoughts but we have to take them captive and make them obedient to God (2 Corinthians 10:5) because that's how you'll free yourself from them. God is graceful and says we can give these to Him because He's not asking you to not be human; He wants to strengthen your human weakness through His superhuman grace. This is so vital and crucial in your strategy.

You are not meandering in the fierce wind aimlessly like a lost piece of paper. You are not a twig being swept by the ocean's will. You are safely in His hands, plan, timing and design. You are rooted and you are anchored. We will find out the "why" in your story once He takes you to where you're going. One day you're going to look back and it will make perfect sense with total purpose. You're going to be rejoicing and victorious. You're going to be stronger, and that much closer to your journey here on earth of inching towards spiritual maturity, lacking nothing. In the meantime, uphold your end of the bargain to your miracle. Focus.

CHAPTER 11

I was a young 27 year old, with no medical experience, diagnosed with the C-word, facing experienced medical experts and staff in white coats, and felt like I was being bullied and opposed by every statistic, piece of jargon and expert recommendation. They were like arrows from the enemy I prayed every day for God to shield me from. I was, to an extent, threatened by some doctors that if I didn't want to necessarily comply at my own will, I would run the risk and would be responsible for it coming back. That's an immense amount of pressure. It was pure turmoil within myself while making these huge decisions. And ironically, the hardest part was that no one else could really make them for me. The decisions fell on me. I felt the weight of the world on my shoulders. I was terrified to make the wrong decision and be responsible if I wasn't here for my family. I felt alone. How could I explain to these medical experts, who felt like giants, that my only evidence as to how I knew their route wasn't for me was what God told me. Mind you, a God, whom many didn't believe in and didn't want to take a chance on.

Your Goliath

Goliath was staring right at me just wanting to completely devour me, taunting me, and walking closer towards me to prove his size. There was one problem: He underestimated my power. On the battle ground, my stature may have been small like David's, but my faith and God's power *within me* dwarfed him. It was an unexpected weapon he would never see coming. I may have been a young, sweet looking 27 year old with no medical degree to the doctors, but the fire in me knew my size was much larger. God spoke David into me (1 Samuel 17).

"You're fully equipped, Airam. I want them to see my might through your petite stature. I want them to see my authority through your young age. I want them to bet against your unwarranted calm poise. I want them to be confused and doubtful in your reckless faith. I want them to call your joy foolish. I want them to stare right in your eyes and see ME staring back. You're bigger, and you're badder, because I am on your side. I AM WHO I AM! Take out your slingshot. Run towards him!"

God Intervenes With Perfect Orchestration

It was time for me and my medical team to meet for our final plan. I compromised that I would not do chemo or radiation before the surgery. I would do the mastectomy on the right breast only, not on my left breast (*in my sureness, I told myself I was and am going to need that baby to breastfeed*), I would do reconstruction on my right, and then we would touch base after the mastectomy when the pathology came back to decide the rest of the course. Remember when I shared about the original surgeon that felt like anything but a match made in heaven? Myself and anyone we had told, prayed and prayed over all my doctors and medical team. In the recurring theme of "coincidence," that general surgeon was not going to be able to perform the surgery on the day I was scheduled for because he was not able to travel to the same hospital that my plastic surgeon does surgeries out of.

Both obviously needed to be available at the same location because while I was under, the general surgeon's job was going to remove the C-word and do everything medically necessary for the best outcome. Then my plastic surgeon would swoop right in and doctor me up to give me the best aesthetically looking breast he could give me. So, as an answered prayer, we needed a new general surgeon.

The date was set for May 1, 2018 and the clock was ticking down. We needed a surgeon fast. There was one surgeon who was available at the hospital we needed and as soon as I got her name, I searched the internet as fiercely as I could to find anything about her. I stumbled upon one review on one of those medical sites and that was it. They mentioned that she did an excellent job at the surgery and said, "She made us feel like actual people." I had a Holy Spirit moment that gave me a knowing, a peace, and hope. She was it. It was time to meet her, and Mikey and I were anxious. It was literally days before the surgery and she was going to be our surgeon no matter what. Finding the right doctors I learned really feels a lot like dating, just way more intense in this case.

As soon as she walked into the room, I knew she was the one. She had an upbeat personality like Mikey and I's, an optimistic aura but with composed intelligence and matter-of-fact way we could trust. She was a person who saw me as a person. She shared with us what she was like, what her interests were, and what her experience was before anything. Honestly, I loved that she was a woman, and not only that, but a woman who had done surgery for other women with the C-word before. I had no clue until she mentioned it. She explained to us that she had already met with the plastic surgeon and board for a game plan and heard a lot about us, that we were a hit with the doctors and staff with our optimism and energy, and that she took her job very seriously. I'll always remember her telling us she liked to go on long runs then get good rest the day before a surgery to gear up for it. She reminded us she was human but I knew in my spirit she was prepared to perform and deliver her very best. She was light but on point. She was who we had prayed for, and who I believed was designed for the job from the beginning.

You Don't Need Easy, You Need Possible

After we had mutually exchanged our good energy and trust, we cut down to business. Because every doctor up until this point had eluded that chemo was the only sane option to guarantee I would be okay, I wanted her to tell it how it was.

"What are we looking for in the outcome to give us the result we want? What are going to be the deciding factors to exactly determine what the next course of action will be? What do we need to see to show I won't be doing chemo? I need to know what to declare when we pray." I wanted bullet points and I was leaning in, looking at her in her eyes.

She looked at me with a tender smile and in her eyes I felt her saying, "*I like your style.*" She flipped over a piece of paper. It reminded me of what Mikey and I call in our business, a napkin presentation. It's when you chicken scratch on a piece of paper but it's powerful, effective, and shows the game plan. She wrote out that during the surgery they would do a separate incision by my armpit and remove some of my lymph nodes. If there was anything in my lymph nodes, I would need chemo. If not, it was a great indication that I would not. She further explained that the next marker was going to be if they got clear margin, meaning nothing questionable left, in the tissue and skin they were going to leave behind. With a mastectomy, they fully remove the breast. All that was going to be left was my skin, which was awesome because I got to keep my nipple which a lot of people aren't able to do. They were going to cut from the side of my breast all the way under towards the inside, and remove the entire breast and what I called the "bad tissue." I oddly envisioned it like an ice cream scoop. Don't ask.

So, after tissue sampling what was left, if there was nothing there, I would be clear. Next, radiation would be dependent on what things looked like once they got in there. She explained that once they were in and could really see what they were dealing with, we would know more. I immediately got excited. I got so excited that I startled Mikey and her. I put my hand on the paper and I leaned in further with a huge smile on my face and I said, "So you're telling me, if I have nothing in my lymph nodes, we get clear margin, and everything looks good, I won't be doing chemo?" She put her pen to her mouth with a smile on her face, leaned back in her chair and gave a cheeky laugh because she was surprised but loved my enthusiasm.

She paused, leaned forward, and looked at Mikey and I. She said, "Look, it's non-aggressive, it's not genetic, and the kind you have will respond to hormone therapy. If this is localized like we believe it is, if there is nothing in the lymph nodes, if the margin is clear, we get in there and by a miracle from a God that seems to be on your side, everything is good, then no, you shouldn't need to do chemo."

I loudly exclaimed, "So you're saying it's POSSIBLE?" with a bold smile. My body was almost out of my seat with my hand on the table and leaned in. She looked at me and I'll never forget it. She had a side smile and a, "*I can't believe I'm saying this yet actually believing this*" demeanor. She said, "2018 could be the year that Airam Batdorf had cancer and you could walk away from this and live the rest of your life as normal."

Bingo. Silence.

I was in the air, slow motion, in the most badass heroine stance, perfect form, releasing my slingshot. The stone was perfectly headed right between the eyes of my Goliath. All I needed to hear was that it was possible. That was all I needed. That's all you need.

I didn't need easy. I didn't need probability. I didn't need an explanation of the chances. I needed possible. Period.

I was going to move that mountain with my mustard seed (Matthew 17:20). The bet was on. God was going to do the "impossible" and I knew it.

A Guarantee From God

I've had people ask me questions before like, "How did you really know He was going to do it? How did you really know He was going to heal you? How are you so sure? How were you so sure the whole time?" Well, my answer is simple: I never 100 percent knew.

We'll never know 100 percent. And, I don't believe at all that God wants us to know 100 percent; then we don't need faith.

When we feel we don't need faith, we forget how much we need Him. Did you know that He wants you to need Him? And not in a way that He wants to tease you or proudly strut in authority over you, even though He does have full authority over the universe. He lovingly and jealously wants you to need Him because He has the power to unlock every beautiful and vast blessing that He so badly wants to give to you. He wants you to need Him; To be close. You know how you have to lean in close in order for someone to hear you whisper? That's how God works. In an intimate whisper. He wants you to have to come closer to hear His voice and sweet sound of promise. He wants you to love Him so you can understand a fragment of how much He loves you. And because He loves you, He wants and knows what's best for you. And more often than not, what's best for us requires us to grow, refine, stretch, mold, and be very uncomfortable. Sometimes we will be in the dark, get buried, change, and expand in the pursuit of faith in God's truth, while in His gracious parameters as a loving father. But, you are not outside of His reach. Although this battle feels far removed in the middle of nowhere, you are safely in the parameters of a loving father that will not give you more than you can bear. You are always at His reach. Every detail of your journey is. Every single detail. Not only that, but He is so near. He is teaching you faith, dear friend. He is stretching your capacity. So meet Him! Meet Him with your faith.

If we had a written promise with guarantee, it wouldn't require faith, and it would not force you to "let perseverance finish its work so that you may be mature and complete, not lacking anything" (James 1:4). I love three words in this verse: "let," "perseverance," and "finish." "Let" implies for us to surrender or to allow; don't fight what God is doing. "Perseverance" implies that we are going to need endurance, so this should not be a surprise in the pain, stretching, and breaking in our process, which He will not just drop you off in, by the way. "Finish" implies that there is an end, a finish line, a goal, a beautiful finished product God has in mind for you, and He says it is lacking nothing. Let this give you hope. You will lack nothing! Other bible versions use the word "perfect." A diagnosis is the perfect arena to mature our spirits to perfection.

So, did I ever get a physically audible voice from above that said, *"You are going to be healed, guaranteed on this day and in this way. I'm going to do A, B, and C and it will never come back?"* No, I never got a factual, written agreement, 100 percent guarantee by human standards. But when I leaned in, real real close, I heard His whisper. His whisper is so soft, but so loud, and you don't hear it from your ears or your head, you feel it in your spirit, as if it's embedding in your every fiber of your being like a soft breeze, and it feels completely calm and at peace.

Go To The Source

I knew, without knowing. How did I confirm I knew without knowing? A couple of weeks into my journey, I stopped asking God every day if He was going to heal me. Instead of asking God every day what He would be willing to do for me, I turned to the Word and I studied every bit of what He did and who He was. And you know what I found over, and over, and over, and over again? Jesus was a HEALER. He healed people all the time. In fact, a broad and considerable amount of the many miracles He displayed that we have record of, were specifically healing. Over, and over, and over again. Of all the things He could do while on Earth- and He did many other miraculous things- for healing to be one of His main objections and prevalent displays of power and mercy, I took it very seriously.

It's proof. It was His nature. He was in the business of healing. It's what He does. The more I frantically searched in the Bible which was my basis for truth, my desperate, fearful frenzy turned to excitement, then later to motivation, and eventually to peace.

Instead of begging God every day to heal me, asking if He would do it, how He would do it and when, I turned to the Word and I used that as my factual, 100 percent, guaranteed evidence as to what God COULD do.

The rest was up to me to believe, declare, and activate in faith; To be bold and reach for His garment. To stand on His rock and His promise for my healing and my future even if I was sobbing, slipping, and barely hanging on to that boulder, not being able to catch my breath.

Keep Your Grip

I'm human and I'd have moments where I would visualize me fiercely struggling to grip the boulder with my body swaying off it's side, looking around and being tempted to ask, "Why can't I let go? Why can't I fall victim like some people do? Can't you just catch me and fix it all? Why can't I heel over and give myself a break? This is hard. I'm tired! You see me struggling. Why do I have to be so strong?"

I never heard an answer to those questions. You know why? Because just like God gives us free will to come to Him, we have free will to be victims or victors. He didn't answer because the answer was within me, and we both knew it. I'd have to ask myself, "Do you want to fall victim Airam? Is that what you want?" My answer was always no. Sometimes it was bold and sometimes it was distraught and kicking rocks like a kid. I'd then hear Him proceed and coach me when I was weakened to get up.

"Focus. You need to use your faith, Airam. Push! Get up. Come on. Again!

Pull yourself up. You're stronger than you think.

I'm your source of strength. Me. Not you. Focus.

Get up. I know it hurts.

Again! I know it's hard. But I am right here. I called you for this.

Finish!"

He was my loud father figure on the sideline during the game or meet. He believed in me. And He knew something within me that I didn't. A force that was wilder than my heart's nudges or imagination.

When you start to know God really well, you know that sometimes He can really kick your butt, in the most loving way possible. I was growing perseverance daily and by the minute, with hope that I was getting closer and closer to the maturity, completion, and perfection He calls us all to. I was storing my treasures in heaven by choosing God over my fear every single day.

I need to share something very important with you: *You are the only one who is going to know what God spoke to you. No one else heard what He told you. And you must, you absolutely must, stand on it. Do not waiver.* You will have moments where your circumstances will look so opposite of His promise, you're anxious for the next test result, the appointments are exhausting and endless, the waiting periods seem like eternity, and you might feel like you're going crazy. Heck, other people might think you're crazy.

You might feel like something just set you back ten strides after you just caught a pace. You'll feel frustrated and fearful that no one else is going to be able to give you the guarantee you want, and the giant will appear bigger and badder. You might go back and forth questioning if God sees you, if He can help you or if He can heal you. You might toggle between what people want to tell you to be realistic about, and the doctors and statistics that might sound definite. Sometimes, you will feel like the bet isn't still on. But my friend, it is! Don't you waiver.

When everything, and maybe everyone, around you says quit, I say get up. This is where you stop fighting the current. Be one with the water. Learn to be still in God. Watch the fierce current start to lose its power as you learn to ride it, float with it, and release your tension. This is where you learn to bob and weave in the ring. You start to step swifter, your hands are quicker, and although bloody and sweaty, you have momentum. The opponent, the enemy, is tiring. But trust me, he's not a quitter either. Stay sharp. It's loud around you but you are focused. Eyes locked. Stance ready. Graceful and lethal at the same time. Focus and endure, my friend. All I needed to know was that it was possible. I am telling you, it is possible. Nothing is impossible with God (Luke 1:37). And you know what? You ARE crazy. Crazy enough to have crazy faith, to see crazy miracles. Own it!

CHAPTER 12

L isten, my bet was *ON*. It was on and I knew it because I claimed it. I had been declaring every fragment of this journey every single day and this was it: The championship match in the ring. This was the pinnacle that was going to decide the rest of the entire trajectory. All the training, all the pain until that point, the sowing of seeds and the belief and faith were going to be manifested in what I believed was us seeing the Lord in a mighty way.

I never told many people this, but in the middle of this journey far before this point, there was a morning that Mikey had left to do some jobs for his business. I was folding laundry at the house in our room by our bed and I was so rid with anxiety and panic I fell to the floor on my knees and I wept. I had my face in my hands and I had my forehead leaning against the side of the bed. I was drowning. I was afraid; my thoughts were all over the place, what-if's were being cast as fiery arrows towards me from the enemy. I was exhausted and I was overwhelmed trying to keep it together. I was having one of the moments where I *"just wanted to know."* I just wanted to KNOW I was going to be okay. That I was going to have a future. That I wasn't going to die. That I'd have my children. That I'd be old and hand-in-hand with my husband watching our grandchildren one day. That my mom's heart wouldn't break if something happened to me. And, that we'd all really see a miracle and I'd know the C-word would never come back. I didn't hear anything at all from God.

The Pinnacle Question

I lifted my head, wiped my tears and I sat up on my knees to pray at my bedside. I was asking God all kinds of questions and going through my declarations through my tears, attempting to make the fear and doubt go away. "Lord, I need you. Please heal me. Work a miracle for us to witness you through me. Please." After a few minutes, I heard the Lord in a way I never expected. It took me by surprise and all that I heard was,

"*And what if I don't?*"

Silence.

"*Why do you want to live Airam?*"

I was alarmed that in my spirit it really was like I heard an audible voice. There was stirring in my spirit and panic in my flesh. I remember pausing and being taken back by such simple but profound questions. The authority and power was frightening, but peaceful at the same time (*that's usually how you know it's God*). Honestly, I look back and think my jaw must have been dropped and eyes wide open thinking, "You better not mess this up girl." He startled me out of the limiting, woe moment.

When God asks *US* questions, that's a serious indicator to humble ourselves, digest what He's asking and use discernment as to why He's asking it. One thing I want to interject here is aside from the initial shock of the question, you do not need to actually fear how you answer. Remember, He already knows what you're thinking before you're thinking it and well before you even consider verbalizing it to Him in your mind or out loud. You are allowed to talk to God without a filter. In fact, I highly encourage it.

So, the God of all the universe, world, time and all existence EVER, says, "*And what if I don't.*" And, proceeded to ask me why I wanted to live. The being who gave me life and had the power to take it away asked me why I want to live. It wasn't in a way to scare me. It was a stern, calm, loving question. Kind of like when a parent or teacher starts with a question because you know they're about to make a really valid point. My tears stopped and I just stared straight ahead. I felt something within me and it was supernaturally distinct, time stopping, and mystical. I couldn't hide from Him. It was as if He was in heaven and the Holy Spirit was supernaturally present in real time, slowly scanning my heart and every fiber within me. And although I didn't give any permission, it didn't feel invasive.

It felt like a sweet white light that had authority as a righteous messenger, mystically moving through me the way smoke moves beautifully and gradually from a wick when it's blown out.

The smoke-like motion was moving throughout my body and being, slowly examining and scanning, creating delicate and mesmerizing patterns. There was no camouflaging or sheltering any part of me, my secret places, my intentions, motives, thoughts, or depths of my heart.

After a minute or two, I looked down and I deflated a little bit. As difficult as it was to say out loud, I knew in my heart what the right answer was and in truth, what I really did feel in my spirit. I quietly said out loud, slowly nodding my head with some tears coming down my cheeks, "If you don't, I will love You Lord. I will still love you. No matter what happens. I love You." At that moment, I knew, He knew that was true. I was afraid to out loud say, "If you don't," but somewhere deep down inside, I felt that this wasn't Him telling me He wouldn't heal me, but more so a test of my heart and a humbling motion to remember that He is the one with the power, the plan, and authority.

My shattered heart was at His feet. Broken at the thought that He's right; He doesn't have to heal me. He didn't owe me anything. It was innocent surrender to Him that I would love and worship regardless of the outcome. I released and humbled myself to the notion at where I stood. I was bowing at His feet; my heart as my sacrifice. As much as it broke me, I felt a peace. I had love in my heart and knew there truly was so much gratitude to have even to this point in my life.

I'm not sure how to say or really explain that it kind of surprised me, but my next answer in my heart and spirit to the question, "Why do you want to live?" was without hesitation. **I wanted to live as a testimony for Jesus.** To be a light-worker. To share healing and faith. I needed to stay because I had unfinished work and even bigger work that hadn't even begun. It came faster than I thought, and it was pure. My heart was truthfully and innocently committed to God and His purposes and plans. I wanted to talk about God for the rest of my life sharing this exact testimony and many others. I wanted to be walking proof that He in present day performs miracles. I felt like I had work to do for Him, purposes that needed to be fulfilled in His glory, and that I was strong enough to do it. I wanted to proclaim how He saved my life not just from the C-word, but how He saved me from the real death; living without fully giving myself to Him. That He is the source, the only source, of true life. I wanted to win others for the Kingdom, and abundantly share the deep treasures I found. I wanted to take up the sword on the battlefield and become a vicious warrior for Heaven.

It was almost as if God took me out of myself and I looked around smiling like, *"What! Did you really just say that and that's the truth Airam?!"* I felt like I passed the test and I was a little kid. Sometimes when we come to the realization of what's inside of us it can really shock us; this surprised me for the better. I kind of laugh thinking about it now. Part of me was surprised I didn't want to live for just more time. I didn't just want to live to do all the things I planned to do all my life, I didn't want to live just to spend more time with my husband even though I loved him more than anything, or my children I dreamed of having. My heart was actually devoted to God. And something deep within me knew, that if I were devoted to God, my biggest gifts and blessings like my husband, my mom and family, children, time, world changing accomplishments, joyous memories, prosperity, abundance, experiences, and other things would absolutely be included. Because these are the beautiful things God gave me in this life. These things are my biggest bonuses in life.

There was nothing but silence, then a whisper.

"I will save you because I know your heart."

I looked up, and I uncontrollably wept. I wept and wept and wept with overwhelming and confused gratitude and humbleness. My hands were stretched out on the carpet and my face was on the ground, creating what I could have sworn was a puddle. I was in awe. I was broken and safely held at the same time. I remember feeling completely overtaken by feeling how mighty God really is; How vast His power and presence is. I was unworthy and He was so good and filled with mercy. I immediately understood that this was an Abraham moment (Genesis 21). He was testing my heart, wanting me to see it, and wanting me to be a witness to my own word. I had been spared in the Hunger Game wilderness during the pinnacle obstacle and rescued from the depths of the black, vicious, raging sea. But, He was nodding at me like, "*We're not done yet. Get going.*" I dusted myself off from the fiery smoke and dirt, and caught my breath from violently swimming, got up and ran as directed.

A lot of the time, our focus is diverted on what's external, when God is actually doing something within us. He is saying what we are looking at and repetitively praying for is already done, and we're missing the real battle. The real point. I wasn't going to save myself. The doctors weren't going to be the ones to save me, although God was going to use them as vital parts of His miracle. I knew He was going to make sure they were going to see Him.

Have you ever known, maybe since you were little, that you were destined for something big? That you were meant to do something revolutionary? That there was something different about you? That was me. And this was it. This was going to be the biggest upset anyone in my possible circumference would see. It was going to be the catalyst for the monumental plans God had for me as a warrior in His army. This was my chance. This was me in the ring, ready to prove every stake God told me I had since I was a child. It was mine. This was every tiny whisper that told me I was the storm when I thought I was in the midst of one throughout my life. This was every tiny whisper within myself that told me the superhero was actually within me, when I didn't have one to fully believe in. Every comment I got my whole life about my potential, the secret I knew I was designed differently, was about to come into fruition like a roaring lion. This was the colossal chance to not just talk about something but truly be about something; to stand for something so much larger than myself. This was for every time I got knocked on my face in my life, getting back up and proving I was worthy.

This was for every time I hated being different and was judged and misunderstood for it. This was honor to the little girl in me I suppressed because I didn't understand why she was different. This was for the same scared little girl to see she was destined to grow up into someone she could be proud of, love, and admire. This was for all the wrong I had done in my life that I didn't need to prove to God I was worthy of forgiveness for, but rather to prove to myself I was redeemed. This was every book, every seminar, every bit of training I poured into myself coming into manifestation like a stored hard drive I had no idea about. This was me willingly being crucified and used as a vessel through myself, my body, my mind and my spirit as a sacrifice to show you who He is; that He would save someone as wretched, sinned, and unworthy as me and still call me perfect and chosen. This was my chance to prove to myself who I was. This was God's opportunity to show me who He was. He had to break me to save me. It was time for me to carry my own cross with His strength. It was time for the surgery.

CHAPTER 13

There we were. I was excitedly anxious to get the bad tissue out of me and get the verdict while nervous at the same time. Up until this point, no one really knew what I was going through besides a few select people. We knew it was time to let everyone in on what our little-big secret was, and what was God's intro as the main event of the show. It was time to set the stage and I knew to be obedient. We started sharing with just our circle of people at the church, we called family members one by one, we told friends, and anyone else that crossed our paths.

<u>Obedience To His Plan</u>

There was one thing I was instructed to do, and it was to ask people to declare with us these specific things, regardless if they believed in God and prayed or not:

1. Covering over the doctors, team and for a great, safe surgery
2. Completely clear lymph nodes
3. Clean and clear margin
4. For God to work a miracle none of us can deny

Of course, everyone empathetically and willingly obliged; some with heavy tears. I knew it was bold. It was extremely bold and intimidating to not only let people in but have people declare something that maybe sounded crazy and would be a huge let down if it didn't turn out that way. But my faith and His assignment was louder. There was a sureness that said, *"Trust me and be obedient."*

I saw what He was doing in setting up His miracle and I needed to obey. I needed to have faith. I was in no position to question Him, and I didn't. In fact, I recruited every person I possibly could to pray. On the day of the surgery, I needed to be at the hospital by 5:45am. I was up at 3am. The house was still. Perfectly quiet. Everything was in place for when it would be time for me to come home: the medications, the special garments I'd need, all the medical supplies, the food, the rearrangements to make things simple, my hospital bag, the things that I was bringing to the hospital to bring me comfort. My mom and Michael were sound asleep. I laid with my eyes wide open staring at the ceiling. I put my hand on my husband's back and I just started to pray. God said, *"One more thing."*

He wanted me to announce, very publicly, what was happening. I immediately was filled with fear and opposition. The stage wasn't fully set. Remember when I said my entire circumference was going to see His glory? He meant that too. I knew this was something I had to do as a piece in His plan that I did not want to get in the way of. I had come this far to not see my miracle. I laid awake, I prayed, and I let Him take over to type whatever He wanted. It was ready to go in my iPhone notes.

Ready As I'll Ever Be, God

It was just Michael and I who drove to the hospital at first. We got in the truck, Mikey and I looked at each other and we had a moment where time stopped for me. We looked at each other in the eyes and both endearingly smiled with closed lips. He grabbed my hand and gave it a squeeze. We were scared, and our eyes kindly told each other so. He put his hand on my lap and I nodded. "Let's do this."

We smiled big and blasted our favorite gospel songs with the sun just barely beginning to make its appearance and sang as loud as we could. We were clapping and swaying, we even opened up the window with the wind fiercely blowing in my face with me yelling out of the side. I looked down and felt the wind in my hair, rushing my face. Within the moment, I felt God and time supernaturally slow down around me like in a movie. The music quieted and I looked at Michael who was still smiling and singing in normal time, but seemed to start moving in slow motion in mine. I closed my eyes. A song called, *"Trust In You,"* was playing and I felt God embracing me in a way I'll never fully be able to describe.

He was quieting my fear, calming my anxiety, and I was imagining me in an all white, open room with no walls and no end with very bright light. In my vision, I was walking towards God and saying, "Well, here we are," with my hands in a W formation and a smile on my face. He was telling me I had done well. He was telling me I was strong and He was proud. That He knew I had it in me. That I had been obedient. He asked me if I was ready. I said, "Ready as I'll ever be."

I was quickly thrown back into the present moment. The sound of Mikey and the music started to come back, time caught up, I opened my eyes, and with intense vigor in them as I was looking straight ahead through the windshield, I heard God say, "*Now.*" I took my typed up proclamation, and pasted it into the box where Facebook says, "What's on your mind?" What was on my mind was me bowing to the Lord's command. I took a deep breath preparing myself to let over 2,000 people into what He was doing, and boldly declaring what He was going to. A lot of people I hadn't seen since high school or college, some were people I was no longer friends with and some were people I was just building relationship with. Some were people that had been seeing me go about my normal happy life at the gym or other places not knowing the whole time this was going on, some were distant family members in other countries, some were people that were literally going to have a wide open window into my intimate life simply because of a random act of friend requesting with no further acknowledgement. I took another deep breath, looked at it, pushed send, and put my phone in my bag. "Ready as I'll ever be, God."

5/1/2018

CHAPTER 13

"Today marks a big day in our journey. Most of you haven't known or don't know, as we kept this tight between close friends and family. I was diagnosed with breast cancer about a month and a half ago. I like to say, I'm "getting rid of the C-word". Let me preface, I have not wanted to share this with everyone both to help keep my mental space and spirit strong, because we didn't and still don't have ALL the answers, and I didn't want to worry everyone. I didn't and don't want people to feel bad for me because I had already seen what God was doing and was going to do from the beginning. This is a victorious story! This is the biggest victory and triumph He chose me as a vessel for. One answer has been here the entire time and remains: God. The way this ENTIRE case has been orchestrated and taken care of can be credited and explained to nothing other than Him. We have been so favored. It would be easy to not share this story and journey to "protect" myself, keep my wall up and just keep the miracle between us, but God cannot move through something or someone unwilling to share what He's done. It is just and right for me to share as I've been prompted. This has been His plan. I will sacrifice a little for God to see me through and for you all to know Him.

Today I am going into surgery to remove what we call in our family, "the bad tissue." We are asking, I am asking, for your prayers. If God did it then, He WILL do it NOW! From the moment I got the call I had an indescribable overwhelming calm and peace that I was okay, and this was going to be okay because the Holy Spirit literally in my entirety has filled me with an unexplainable assurance to take me through that I couldn't understand myself, and showed me from the VERY beginning that this was already finished. I knew what God was using this for. I knew what He was going to do. I knew this journey wouldn't be just about me, this was being used to share with you from the very beginning. And so, I have fully given the reigns to Him. This is setting the stage for God. And I promised to share and give every bit of this glory and praise to Him because it is the truth.

And so I let go and give this piece to Him as I let you all in to watch what He is going to do. The miracles He has already worked and will continue to work have left us in awe. I welcome you to not have fear and to be encouraged as I have, with absolutely no credit to myself but to only God guiding my every moment and piece of this journey.

I want to tell you all is good! I am good, we are good, and we are SO blessed! I truthfully and supernaturally haven't had one ounce of true fear and have never felt more joy, calm and confidence in my entire life. This experience has resurrected my soul and changed my life for far far better and has prepared me to be used by Him. One day, this will all be just a piece of God's greater plan. One day and throughout my dedicated and long life, as I share more of this testament with the world, I will see *this all full circle and so will you. We will see Victory and nothing short!"*

The Match

We got to the check in station on the floor we were supposed to be at and the nurse immediately knew who I was. She was sweet, and for whatever reason, I felt like she was the first angel I had been meticulously envisioning day after day for how this day was going to go, down to every detail. Our family pastor at our church so graciously met us to pray with us and the nurse winked at me and said, "You know what, you go ahead and you use that room right there." I knew she wasn't supposed to let us, but she did. When we prayed with our pastor was angel number two.

I couldn't remember exactly what was said but I remember I immediately felt confirmation everything was moving carefully and divinely into place. I was in the zone and everything around me felt peace and covering. It was indisputably like déjà vu, playing out exactly how I imagined it down to how I would feel. When we walked out of the room, my best friend and my mom had arrived and it was time for me to go to the waiting area which was where I would dress down and I'd have my own bed and curtained off area until it was my turn to get rolled back. The room had everyone else who was waiting for their surgery in their own curtained off section too, somewhat like a parking lot. It for whatever reason seemed to bring comfort to me while wondering what surgery they were going to get done. Mikey, my mom and best friend were in the tiny space with me. We were all keeping it light and positive. My best friend was playing worship music from her phone really quietly and they were trying to keep me entertained.

The Bones

I could tell my nerves were kicking in and my focus was intense. I was talking less and less by the minute. My phone was going crazy now that the world knew but I dare not look. *"Focus on me Airam,"* is all I kept hearing. My best friend said, "Oh my gosh! I randomly painted my nails yellow today!" We giggled that my socks matched her nails. I randomly wore these yellow socks that I never wore, that always sat at the bottom of my sock drawer. I remember thinking that yellow was a happy and joyful color so I decided to put them on before we left. The doctor came in and went over what was going to happen in terms of the surgery and anesthesia. It all sounded so simple really. Kind of how God's promises sound at first. He lays it all out in the beginning and every time it sounds so simple. Like, *"Hey, Airam...I know you just got told you have the C-word but don't worry! You're going to be totally fine, I'm going to miraculously heal you then I'm going to use you and this testimony for my glory in more ways than you can wrap your head around. Trust me, ok?"*

Those are the bones. That's the rock. God doesn't give all the in-between partly because I believe we would totally mess up His plan; partly because I believe we can't fully handle everything at once so He graciously gives us little by little, but also because, this is how we persevere in our faith, remember? That was kind of how they explained the surgery.

"We've got to take you back, inject radioactive glowing blue stuff through your nipple while you're awake with something that looks like a horse tranquilizer, so that we can map from your glands to your lymphs to make sure they're clear. Then we're going to take you back and inject your spine with nerve block, again with a horse tranquilizer, so you're as numb as your body can handle for the surgery. Then we're going to get you into the operating room; your general surgeon is going to go in, remove the C-word and your breast, then your plastic surgeon is going to swoop right in and reconstruct it with the implant and fix it up. Should take four to five hours and then you'll wake up! Ready? Break!"

Okay, I'm being a bit facetious and over-kill with the horse tranquilizer but that's basically how it went. However, the technicality, precision, timing, orchestration, amount of steps, and procedure are obviously not that simple when actually executing a surgery- *just like the in-between's of your plan.* After getting the nerve block in my back, my body was numbed and I was already fading in and out and at this point I was on my own; no family around me. There was a nurse rubbing my back and telling me I was so sweet and brave like an angel. She felt like an angel to me. Things were blurry and the team moved fast. As I was wheeled down the hallway I could see the bright hallway lights blinding me on and off as I passed them. I remember them bringing me into the operating room. There were tons of bright lights in the round room, they counted to three and lifted me on to the table. A mask was put on my face and as the nurse was rubbing my hair, she asked me to count down from ten. Every second became more faint for me to even say the word, "Jesus."

I don't remember anything passed four.

Sweet Promise

Waking up, I literally remember thinking, "Am I dead or alive?" I was still so out of it from the extremely high pain medication I was on. I opened my eyes to extremely bright lights right above my face. I was alive! The nurses came right over and they rubbed my hair and we smiled to each other. Even though I felt nauseous and out of it from the medication, I remember rejoicing and thanking the nurses over and over again. I was so loopy and the come down from the medication started to give me an anxiety attack. They cracked a potent essential oil stick under my nose and it grounded me.

I was asking how everything went and they told me everything went great, we laughed and praised in gratitude. I got carted out and my family was right outside of the room. They ran right over and all kissed me and were thrilled. My best friend turned to me and she said, "Guess what! They had this screen in the waiting room that had color coded lights to tell us what part of the process you were in. And they told us that when it goes to yellow, it means you're done and everything is good! It must not be an accident! Yellow is our color today," with a big smile on her face. I believe in the magic of little moments like this. I will forever love those yellow socks and although they have holes now, I'll never toss them because of the joy and tiny reminder they are that God is God and that miracles are real.

My sweet mom and husband were preparing to set up shop: Jimmy rigged beds in the room to never leave my side and they made sure I was okay. The room we got actually had a big window, with beautiful buildings outside and a church with a cross at it's roof's peak. The next morning, there was this sunrise like I had never seen before. It was pure peace with purples, oranges, yellows and deep blues and all you could see most prevalently was that tall cross. I was still mostly motionless but Mikey and I were playing Frank Sinatra, smiling and singing with each other. And then, everything slowed down. It was slow motion again.

I had been envisioning that exact moment for weeks, and under my breath, I said what I had been telling myself I would say, with the same emotion I felt before it even happened: "He did it." It was so much sweeter than I had imagined.

The surgeons told us it could take up to two weeks to get the pathology back. So, it was time to head home, heal and wait. Three days later, I was sitting in front of the window and my mom was fixing me some food and tea while Mikey was out on a few jobs. I was staring outside with my favorite blanket and my Bible when my phone rang. It wasn't a number I recognized but I picked up. I heard a frantic voice that said, "Airam? It's Dr. Harper." It was my general surgeon. I couldn't figure out why she was calling me and my heart immediately dropped.

This was only three days after my surgery. She wasn't supposed to be calling. Let alone, why was *she* calling me? It's usually never the actual surgeon calling you but rather a nurse or attendant. She continued, "Are you sitting down? Is Michael with you?" She was excitedly panicked and my head was still spinning.

"Yes I'm sitting down. No, he's not but my mom is with me... is everything ok?"

She proceeded to say out of breath, "I only have a quick minute, I am in the middle of a surgery but in passing I got a quick glimpse of your pathology reports. They came in way earlier than we expected. I needed to call you!"

My first thought was, "*OMG you're calling me in the middle of a surgery?!*" My heart was beating out of my operated chest and I, in pain, stood up. Do you remember the four things we asked everyone to pray for? The surgery went the best it could have gone and my team was absolutely amazing, so Number One was already answered. Then, like déjà vu out of movie, she excitedly (*in order I might add*), said,

"Your lymph nodes came back negative and clear." (*Number Two*)

"We tested and we have completely clean and clear margin." *(Number Three)*

And, you're not going to believe this. I just don't know how to explain this. Remember how we saw that the mass was over 5cm? It *shrunk!* What we took out was only a little over 3. We don't understand how this happened, this does not happen." She was energetically confused and shocked. She proceeded, "I don't think you understand what that means! You won't be needing radiation because this puts you under the 5cm benchmark and although it's between you and the oncologist, you probably won't need chemo. We got this out." *(Miracle Number Four)*

My hand covered my mouth, I was shaking and I was speechless. We shouted and rejoiced on speaker phone together and my mom was jumping up and down for me in tears. "I have to get back to my surgery now. I will talk to you soon.

Hey, Airam? Congratulations," she said.

I was quiet in disbelief and if my body wasn't in so much pain I would have collapsed to the floor on my knees. I couldn't speak or shed a tear at this point. For the first time in my life, I was truly speechless. Numbers two, three, and miracle number four happened. They happened! My mom saw me inch myself towards the living room without a sound. She said, "What's wrong? Aren't you happy?" I looked at her and my eyes were now completely filled with tears and I just said, "He did it." I was so overwhelmed with gratitude I was frozen. She gently hugged me and said, "Anak, that's God's grace. You deserve this." She then proceeded to jump, shout and praise God on her knees. With her rejoicing in the background, I looked at the same picture frame with the photo of Michael and I on our wedding day, in the exact same spot as the day I received the diagnosis call. It all came full circle, and it was so divine.

CHAPTER 14

He did it. He healed me by the bold touch of His garment. He healed me with the faith I brought. He healed me with the surrender I left at His feet. He healed me with the prayers of the hundreds of people watching. But He wasn't done.

Exceedingly, Abundantly Above All We Ask or Think

A few weeks after the surgery I had my follow up appointment with the oncologist to come up with the game plan for further treatment based off of the surgery and pathology. There was an important lesson here for me.

Sometimes we want to proclaim things are finished before God says it's complete.

Actually, we do this a lot of the time. We looked at the miracle from the surgery and we were ready to call the match. My opponent was down in the ring. Everyone was cheering for the win. But God said, not yet. I was indescribably happy, humble and floored with gratitude, but admittedly was a little impatient, thinking to myself, "*It's over now... right? Can we be done now?*" I knew to fall back and take His lead. My body healed to such a high degree and so quickly that the oncologist couldn't tell that I had the surgery. I had even gone on a moderate hike two weeks after. We walked in and he was shocked. "You DID have the surgery right?" He double checked the charts.

Although I was incredibly grateful for God's favor in my healing, I wanted to cut to the chase. Where we had left off was him fighting for me to still do the chemo and full time span of hormone therapy. I don't like to believe that he was a villain only out to get me to do whatever means of oncology I'd agree to. He was doing his job but God empowered me to be firm. Although we had a fairly good relationship, it was always back and forth between us. Two bulls who knew the other wasn't fully going to back down but open to hearing one another.

During this visit, we were going to specifically discuss the Oncotype Test's score I got from the pathology, whose results I hadn't heard anything about yet. An Oncotype Test is what happens when they take the physical tumor they remove and they send it to a special lab that runs it's DNA as if it's a human. It takes it's biology like a person, and finds out its genes and what it likes, what it doesn't like, what its specific traits are, what it feeds off of, paired with what your genes and demographics are, then spits out a number from 1-100 that quantifies your recurrence risk and whether chemotherapy will benefit you. For reference, getting anything under about a 26 is considered low-risk chance at it ever recurring.

The doctor was of course happy for such astounding and unexplainable results from the surgery, but he still had a job to do and a specific perspective based off his expertise. He was confused and taken back that the tumor had shrunk, and Mikey and I were preparing ourselves to state our case based on what we viewed as an evident miracle God worked. He said he was going to grab the Oncotype results and he took a long while.

When he knocked on the door to come back in, his face was white. He honestly looked like he had seen a ghost and he was running his hands through his hair, scratching his forehead and stopped dead in his tracks with the door still open. He looked straight at me in my eyes, shut the door, shook his head and said, "I don't think you're from this planet. If there is a God, he is definitely working for you." Mikey and I looked at each other completely confused, thinking he was still talking about the miracle God worked through the surgery. We weren't expecting at all what happened next.

The doctor sat down, put the piece of paper on the table face down, took his finger and pushed the paper towards us. I looked at him and hurriedly took the paper; the score was a 0. *Impossible. Zero.* My heart was racing, and he interjected before I could even say anything. "Airam, in all my years of medical study and medical practice, I've never seen anything like this. I didn't even think this was possible. I don't know how this is possible. None of us have ever seen this before."

It was like you would hear a pin drop in the room if it did. My eyes slowly looked up at the doctor and all I heard in my mind was the slow motion contact of my glove on the enemy's jaw.

Knockout.

God miraculously worked a miracle none of us could deny. I only got the mastectomy on my right breast, never needed the chemo, and never needed the radiation. What I never believed to be in my plan, was in fact not.

Get Out Of His Way

Remember how my life was largely centered around personal development in the beginning? Many people throughout my journey said things like, "If there's anyone I know could beat it, it would be you." A lot of people naturally attributed the fact that I beat it based on my ambition, Michael and I's lifestyle centered around personal development, my positive attitude and go-getter personality type. And, in truth, I believe those things definitely prepped me and contributed in their own respect. But I need to make one thing clear:

This season taught me that personal development can only take us to a certain degree because personal development is centered in the "I" mentality.

It's centered in our own capabilities. I still love to spend time bettering myself with personal development books, self-help Audibles, seminars, you name it. I believe they're beneficial as positive tools towards mental growth, professional growth, performance, finances, emotional awareness, healing, marriage, life skills, relationships, and more. However, this taught me an incredibly valuable lesson. God didn't want me to focus on my abilities at all. He was stretching me to believe in His. He broke off every bit of self-reliance while building me up to become ruthless at the same time. My only job was to keep having faith and return to the home post when I wandered away.

My abilities alone weren't going to fulfill the journey, the molding or the stretching. My own earthly abilities weren't going to be solely responsible for the supernatural miracles. My own strength wasn't going to get me through the grueling fight. I couldn't pull myself out of the depths of the deadly sea; God's hand needed to pull me out. My skills and personal development kept me in the game, but God is who called the shots and made things happen. The strength you all saw was His, manifested in me. I had to learn surrender when all I knew was to push in my own strength prior. God wanted me in a position where I would need to rely on His strength and abilities, not my own, without choice. He wanted me in a position where other people wouldn't be able to deny it was Him. This is how He works. He wants His glory known, and it usually comes in the form of us surrendering our will, our plan and our power. Your power in this world comes from allowing God to overtake you to give you His. And I have good news: His is Almighty and limitless. Why would you want to solely rely on only your own?

You will be called to do the walking, the building and the doing but God is the One in control and orchestrating. I watched the newly released Harriet Tubman movie and a quote that shook me the most was, "Don't tell me what I can't do. God was watching, but my feet were my own." Yes, give yourself the credit and validation that you are hanging on, doing the work, and pushing through. Be proud of yourself, because God is proud of you! But always know that God is the master orchestrator. This defined what I experienced and what I believed.

I sure did walk through the trench. I sure did go through the dangerous wilderness, adventure and obedience myself. I gasped for air and swam with all my might in that thunderous sea. I fought in the ring; learned every move and mastered the grace and sting. I sure did carry something physical within my body. I went through the long days and endless nights, having to choose to fight and win battles no one saw. I went through the surgery, a whole part of my body was removed, I navigated through my life and went through the grueling, resurrecting, excruciating, molding and shaping of myself. But although it was my feet on the ground, it was God's hands and His grace guiding me and shaping everything around me.

To the outside world it looked like an effortless expedition. I heard that a lot. But, it's because God is not someone you can physically see. When they were applauding my strength, it was really God's strength that was being embodied through me which you can physically see in our dimension. I give God all the credit for the miracle, and I give myself the credit for moving out of the way and being obedient. For this, God rewards me in so many more important ways than receiving credit.

So, what do we classify as "seeing God?" Going through the C-word and the way He wanted to show Himself through me showed me that when I look with a different lens, I can physically see God all around me. Sometimes I can see Him in situations or other people, and sometimes it's the way the breeze moves through the trees really gently while I'm praying on my sunrise walk. You can see Him too, if you look closely.

Surrender

Get very familiar and great at surrender. Usually when the word surrender comes up, the next word that comes to mind is "weak." Surrendering could be seen as giving up power in this world; a world where we are constantly taught to fight for power. In this world, giving up power could mean to give someone or something else advantage over you; to give away your strength or to give up. But what if you gave your power away to the person who actually holds all the power in the universe and He says, *"Transfer your power to me and I will show My power through you. I'll fight for you. I am on your side and will fight all your enemies, fears and doubts. I will fight your battle to guarantee victory."* Is that really giving up and surrendering power if by giving up your power you are backed by the one person who will make you win anyways? Easier said than done, and from personal experience, surrender is the hardest thing humans can do. Why? Because surrendering is the most unnatural thing to us. We are built and taught to survive. It takes unprecedented courage to surrender because we have to give up control. Your power lies within surrender because that is where you will gain access. The more you can learn to disarm the notion that you can, will or have to do it all, you realize that His strength overpowers yours, fights on your behalf and moves, shifts and shapes things like you wouldn't believe.

I Understand Why Now, God

Earlier in the book, I encouraged you through my strategy and revelation to never ask God, "why," because He will reveal that to you later in the process. Successful people with great stories are always successful because of how they overcame adversity. The thrill and triumph in the story, along with the credited heroic stature of these people, wouldn't be anything without the circumstance or place of difficulty to prove how they prevailed. You don't get victory without some kind of battle or test. Everyone wants the champion story but they don't fully take into consideration the inner work, metamorphosis, dedication, pain, breaking, sacrifice, and tears that it may require. Or, they don't fully internalize what they're asking for. That included me. I underestimated the price of suffering. It taught me a valuable lesson in the suffering Jesus willingly partook in for our lives and salvation.

My husband's background is filled with evident adversity. I always admired his eagerness for resiliency and looked up to his will to overcome. I still do. There were numerous times we'd be talking and I'd innocently joke that it wasn't fair that he had such a powerful testimony to share with people and that I'd never had it that bad. Do you remember how a lot of the theme of this book is to be careful about what you think and speak? And, about what you believe internally? You're connecting the dots of what God transpired, aren't you?

To ring in the New Year of 2018, I did a fast that our church always does to start the year off on the right foot. This was January, a few short months before I was diagnosed. You will find many powerful examples of fasting within the Bible and so we follow Jesus' lead within our faith walk. Fasting is essentially giving up food, or whatever parameters you set, for a period of time in order to focus your thoughts on God and your spirit. By depriving our flesh, we can hear the Spirit and God more clearly, we can see the condition of our spirits, and we devote ourselves to worshipping and prayer towards an important cause.

That New Years, I remember feeling lost as to what my purpose was. I was seeking and constantly asking, "What am I supposed to *do* in this life? What should I be doing?" Other than that, I just remember thinking, "God, I just want to hear you. Anything." One morning, there I was, standing at my stove making tea, my left foot propped on my right calf, with worship music playing on my phone. Does this stance sound eerily familiar to the beginning of the book?

Being a few days into my fast, I felt like I was getting absolutely nothing other than my body feeling refreshed and being fairly hungry. No messages received, hadn't heard anything monumental and life-changing from God, no answers to my questions; just silence. As I was standing there listening to that worship song, I was overwhelmingly taken by this rush of emotion and I just started to weep out of nowhere. I mean, completely sobbing at the stove. Something dawned on me in that very moment that clearly came from the Holy Spirit: "I've never on my own actually gotten on my knees to pray." It was as if something was physically pulling me to my knees and I slowly lowered, putting one knee then the next on the ground. Then, my arms uncomfortably but almost out of my control, slowly raised overtaken by the song and a powerful euphoria and despair at the same time. Once in that position, my face covered in tears and snot, the music seemed to quiet and I heard a loud, practically audible voice: *You ask so many things of Me. You bring your every need, every care, every problem, every request and every question. I love you, hear every one, and always provide. After all that, there is only one thing I ask of you: to worship Me.*" Wow. I collapsed like a baby.

He was right. Really. Think about it. We bring so many things to God every single day. The big and the small. And He delivers! He comforts, answers, changes, provides, calms, heals, fixes, revives, forgives, protects, loves, listens and strengthens us around the clock, without fail, without question.

Even through our sin and failure. And, even when we heartbreakingly forget about Him. And yet, He asks one thing of us: to simply worship Him.

Wow. I was rocked by a large wave I didn't see, that harshly took me and twirled me for a minute under water then spit me back out to safety on the sandy beach with my stringy hair tousled in my face and catching my breath. It felt like a spanking. But, how true? How valid is that?

Although I had been walking in my faith for years, been baptized, gave my life to Christ, and attended church regularly, it was that moment that I gave my purpose to Christ. It was that moment that I realized my purpose will never be in what I do, but who I serve. My life was His to use, dedicated to worshipping Him. I stopped asking and started listening. Little did I know, in that very same spot, in the very same manner, alone with God, would I find one of the biggest surprises of my life just two months later; I found the lump in my breast.

When I said I was ready to go and willing to do, I wasn't expecting it to come in the package it did. But it came; perfectly timed, with an oddly perfect-sense explanation, and a big obligation. This was the battle to give me the triumphant story I always joked I wanted, the initiation into the champions club, and the proof that God trusted me with my word. He had a purpose for me all along. I underestimated who I was and what I was sent here to do. He's good, isn't He?

Pick Up Your Mat

One of my favorite Bible stories within John 5 is when Jesus is in Jerusalem at the Bethesda pool. This pool is where very many sick, disabled, blind, or paralyzed people would lie. There was one man in particular who had been there for 38 years. Jesus notices him in his terrible condition and that he had been there for so long. He approaches the man and asks him a simple question: "Do you want to be healed?" When Jesus asks the man, "Do you want to be healed?" the man wasn't immediately like, "*YES! OF COURSE! I'VE BEEN WAITING!*" Instead, the man answers Jesus by saying, "Sir, I have no one to put me into the pool when the water is stirred up, and while I am going another steps down before me" (John 5:7).

This man doesn't realize it at that moment, but Jesus is offering him freedom and healing, and the man is focused on the limitations. It was all he knew and all he had seen. He was consumed by the problem that he couldn't embrace the miraculous possibility right in front of him. *We have a choice: focus on limitations or embrace possibility.*

It is such a simple question Jesus asks, yet the man has a complicated response. How often is God asking us a simple question, and we give a complicated response? The complication comes because we don't understand how simple God is when He makes a promise. Jesus is straight up and deliberately asking us,

"Do you want to be healed?"

"But Jesus, they told me that this is impossible. The statistics all show that this turn around is unlikely. They are giving me no alternative. Nothing is working. Everything around me looks the opposite of that. That test said otherwise. We've tried that already. My life is falling apart. We don't have the means for this. My family is breaking. I can't do another round. I had my hopes up already. You don't understand. It's not that simple, Jesus."

Jesus asks the man one question for a reason. Because with Him, it is that simple. I believe Jesus is asking us, *"What's the real issue here, child?"* Is it that we don't fully believe? That deep down, we aren't willing to give up control? That we don't want to make room for Him? Do you really want things to change? Are you ready to take on the armor of responsibility if He heals you?

What straightforward question is Jesus asking you in your life right now?

We think that the man is silly for not immediately answering, "Yes, of course," to Jesus. And you might think your immediate answer would be yes. But would it? Is it? Is your answer immediate and with expectancy? Or is it delayed, meek, and filled with the loss of hope, "38 years worth" of waiting, and reasoning as to why it can't or probably won't happen?

Right after the man tells Jesus that he has no one to put him in the pool, Jesus says nothing other than telling him to "get up, take (his) mat, and walk. At once, the man was healed, and he took up his mat and walked" (John 5:8-9). Jesus is virtuously patient. However, when I read that text, I feel a sense of bother in the man's lack of faith. I sense a loving reprimand that says, "*Stop limiting what I can do. Stop underestimating what your faith is capable of.*" He is asking you today, "Do you want to be healed?"

Pick up your mat and walk.

What do you believe, and who do you believe in? See, my belief in God was much larger than a diagnosis. I believed and still believe God when He said, "*I need you to trust Me. Everything is going to be okay.*" Now, as a pre-warning, I'm not saying that everyone is going to have the exact experience I did, that God is going to heal the exact same way, or that He's telling you the same thing in the same manner. All I know is that you do have the power to choose what you believe, and this makes all the difference. You have a God who is on your side. You have supernatural abilities within yourself to fight that are not of "might" because He is in you. You have access. Healing is yours. Joy is yours. Strength is yours. Miracles are yours. And your body will fall to the command and authority of your mind and spirit if you allow your mind and spirit to fall to the authority of God.

When writing this book, I questioned if this would be "too much." What is going to be too much when talking about God? What do people want to hear? When God finally said, "Go," to writing this book, the questions stopped. I saw God, it was silent, and there was the loud, powerful whisper, "Go." The atmosphere shifted, and the words wouldn't stop. My job and obligation are to give you the knowing that you are an overcomer because of the One who came before you. He is fighting for you, He is for you, and He wants to use you. I want you to experience the power of accessing the miraculous, superhuman realm. To be awed at how He can move and work miracles by the hour, half-hour, and minute. He wants to carry you through the "here and now" in mighty, unexplainable ways so that you can realize that the "above" is actually right here, in front of you, where you are. Will you let Him in?

PART 2

When going through the C-word, I sought information aligned with what God put in my heart to explore, which was anything and everything centered around healing and thriving. I not only wanted to find wisdom on how to heal what was within me or the environment that created it, since I believed that my body wasn't "sick," I wanted to learn how to fuel it for strength and optimal thriving. I compiled information aligned with my holistic beliefs that were scientifically-backed or proven from someone else's life experience. I fostered certain principles and teachings from others; some were famous and accredited, some were survivors, and some that I simply just found wise. And, collectively, I created principles I generated on my own. I meshed my love for personal development and mental fitness with physical fitness, nutrition, meditation, faith, and many other things that inspired me or spoke to me. It's what worked for me with gracious guidance from the Lord.

My experience and advice are not intended as a substitute for the medical advice of physicians. Consult your physician team as your soundboard regarding any diagnosis or symptoms you may have. However, as Deepak Chopra says when talking about the mind-body connection, "It's okay to believe the diagnosis, but you do not have to believe the prognosis." Do what is right for your unique situation, body, inner and outer health, and God's plan for you. I genuinely believe that these principles do not apply to just breast cancer or any cancer, but health and abundance in the mind and spirit for anyone, sick or not. You can apply the essence of specific situations here, to the situations and mindsets within you life. In briefly sharing some of my methods, I hope to give you much of what I sought after when I felt scared and alone. I still use many of these today and will continue to use them while continuously adding to my arsenal. I encourage you to not limit yourself to what I did, but to use this to encourage you to expand your thinking, beliefs, and resources, to create a path tailored perfectly for you. In my purpose of this book, it's essential for me to share my approach in mindset, spirituality, and some of my tactical game plan so that you can use all, or a piece, towards your healing or life approach. You are not to blame for where you are at if you are in a health crisis, but you have the power to create change. I want you to know and believe that you do. Here we go.

Going To Appointments

Appointments. They're frequent and can be scary. Typically, you're going in to get some sort of test done or receiving a result. It's an uneasy stepping stone you have no choice to leap on, yet you anxiously await them when scheduled. I get it! Appointments are part of the process. In circumstances when we don't have a choice, we absolutely have a choice with our approach. Appointments in this particular circumstance we cannot avoid. My choice was to leverage appointments to grow, intentionally find joy, spread joy, positivity, and share Jesus. It was either that or be completely overridden with dread, skepticism, and melancholy.

I became intentionally expectant at what they would look like, the energy I would receive, the energy I would give, and the results I would get. I was learning to shape my trajectory with my belief and the legit possibility that I could actually do that. The notion that that was possible came from personal development and Biblical teachings that thoughts are things. One of my favorite books I read that taught me this was The Secret by Rhonda Byrne. What you envision will happen, and whatever you put out in words, actions, thoughts, and emotions, you're going to receive. I'd sit and visualize what an appointment would look like every day leading up to it. I'd envision even down to what they would feel like, what the results would sound like, and my emotional reaction as a mental rehearsal. Since I already knew I had to go to an appointment, a fun game I'd play was seeing how many people's days I could brighten with a smile. Or, shock them with God's graceful peace and unexplainable joy that I would happily tell them was from Him.

Based on my earlier writing, it's important to remember that this capability was not just mine. You'd be shocked at how many people continuously and without fail would say, "Well, how do you do that? How are you so calm? How are you so positive? What do you do?" Appointments became an opportunity for me to freely say His name without immediate discomfort or questioning. Like I mentioned before, there's a natural openness that people want to give and have when you're going through the C-word. People didn't question me too much. They gave me the floor, whether out of empathy, loss of words, respect, or adoration. So, I used that "power" to further the purpose of however God wanted to present Himself in that moment or to that person, not to receive sympathy. It gave me a purpose in setting the stage for God's ability and willingness to use me, rather than falling to the dread of the appointment or lack of control in the situation.

It gave me a fortunate, beautiful window to share His given peace and joy with others, and I seriously loved that. It gave me a powerful gift of humble joy in these appointments and the day-to-day. It filled my spirit and gave me hope. No one expects effortless and radiating joy, let alone comfort, during tragedy. I didn't even expect it, but the Lord was gifting me with it, and I wanted to share that with others because it wasn't just mine to keep. Being the unexpected grew to be something I loved. The more positive, joyous, and calm I was, the more people saw God without me having to do or say anything. They were confused, puzzled, and shocked that I wasn't anxious or in fear. And the thing was, that I knew in my core that Jesus was the only explanation I had for that. I knew He gave me total peace on purpose because I gave Him faith first and was a willing vessel. The more I leaned in, the more He supplied me with calm. And I desperately needed calm.

Whether going to medical appointments or not, how can you lean on God for more peace and joy in those situations you dread or the tragedy you are going through? How could God use you here? Think of where you can make room to allow Him to come in and give you "illogical" joy, peace, and calm. Going to the plastic surgeon's office were some of my favorite appointments. You know how some people take their job very seriously and it seems like they forget they're human sometimes? Come on. I know you know what I'm talking about. There's a work personality Janet, and then there's outside of work Janet that you run into at a restaurant or the grocery store. You finally see them for the humanity that's actually in them. I found it satisfying to bring fun Janet out with a playful personality.

Can you imagine what happens to most people when they look at your chart, and the first thing they notice is the C-word at age 27? It felt like they prepared themselves to be super reserved and almost melancholy in anticipation that that's what I would be. Call my personality big, but everyone's inner Janet came out in that office by the time I was healed. It was remarkable, gratifying, and fun. I loved it. My plastic surgeon was a deliberate guy that took his job very seriously. He was professional, put-together, factual, meticulous, and timely. But, I knew he wasn't all that serious inside.

I'll never forget the first day we met. He started asking some lifestyle questions. "How are you feeling? What do you do for fun? Do you exercise?" His straight and stern posture began to relax a little as he heard Mikey and I's upbeat personalities, interests, and lifestyle. He proceeded to say, "I mean, you seem like you're doing really well. I'd never know that you're going through what you're going through." I'll never forget when he smiled a little confused and leaned forward as his voice softened.

"You're really not stressed?"

"No."

"You're not anxious?"

"Nope."

"You're not... depressed?"

"No! Do I look depressed?"

"Well, no. Most people usually are, though. How do you do that?"

"God! God, and A LOT of working out," I winked.

"Huh...."

Throughout our growing relationship, I found that all the staff started to tell us that he would mention to them that we were his favorites because we were high energy, upbeat, friendly, and joyful. And on another note, when you go through breast cancer specifically, you get comfortable taking your top off with countless people seeing your breasts. You kind of have to find a light heart. Often, I'd have to get physically examined or have pictures taken in front of everyone. I mean, yeah, it's weird at first. Still, after becoming closer and closer with the staff, appointments oddly became like reunions with good friends. We'd hoot and holler at how great my breasts were going to look, tease with my husband about going to nude beaches, laugh hard and hug. The staff would say, "*We can't handle you!* You are our favorite. We just love you!" And my husband would say, "That's my wife." That's a heck of a lot better than dreading the appointment from my standpoint. The emotion I was receiving was the emotion I was manifesting and putting out.

Another time, we were leaving an appointment, and Mikey and I had smiles from ear to ear the length of the Mississippi River. We were practically skipping holding each other's lower backs while walking, leaning into each other. There was a sweet older couple waiting for the elevator, and they were fixated on us. They were adoringly gazing at us in curiosity about why we were so happy. I smiled and said, "Hello!" They smiled and said, "Well, hello! You two are just absolutely glowing. You look like you got some good news. Are you pregnant?"

He leaned in a little with the adorable smile old grandpas give. I smiled and sighed at such a humbling, sweet thought, and laughed at the bluntness. "I wish that were the case!" They looked at us like, "*Well, are you going to tell us or what?*" Mikey told them we just left the plastic surgeon's office, and the older gentleman said, "Oh! Okay, well, we won't ask. Ya'll just look so happy." He probably thought I was going to get my boobs done or something (*I'd so insert the half sideways smile emoji for my pun*). I *was* going to get my boobs done, and we had just gotten great news. The older man didn't know that the day before, we found out the C-word in my body wasn't genetic. This meant I could keep one of my breasts instead of removing both of them. I linked being able to keep my breast as a sweet sign that I would breastfeed one day.

I had an over joyful hope for future pregnancies we actually would be glowing about one day because of that answered prayer. I'd get to breastfeed my babies from the body that was undergoing what this sweet couple would never expect. They didn't understand that my left breast felt like I was hugging something "I got to keep," like a child hugs a stuffed animal tightly with their eyes closed and a comforted smile on their face. These were very real miracles for me. These were things I specifically prayed for that I saw in real life, in real-time. God was embracing me, and I was feeling His unsurpassed love in ways you can't explain. I smiled and told the sweet couple it was just the Lord's glow. How many things in your life could be a lot more enjoyable by merely changing your perspective?

Another considerable aspect of appointments or other challenging circumstances is that you're going to face a lot of people, staff, or doctors that understandably may or may not know how to interact with you because of what you're going through. They mostly likely are projecting how they think is best to act or how they themselves would act. Let's give them grace here. However, although we are giving them grace, energy is real and shouldn't be taken lightly. You have two options: You can walk in and be at the mercy of their energy or humbly adjust the room with yours and have them meet you. I believe we are not above doctors, but we are not beneath either. I visualized operating as a team with my staff, giving their best care and flowing, good energy. I genuinely believe that if you are feeling bullied by your doctors, the synergy is off. Still, it's equally important not to subscribe to the channel headlined, "Every doctor is a bad villain and out to get me."

Please don't because it's not true. And to put it bluntly, if you do, that's what you're going to get.

Do not go into your appointments with anger or suspicion. Go in ready to give the benefit of the doubt and opportunity for teamwork in your miracle. I prayed before every appointment, asking God to fill me, prepare me, guide my spirit, protect my heart, safeguard my mind, and allow me to be used in whatever capacity He had for that day and appointment. I chose to believe every meeting was either going to challenge me to lean into God on more profound levels or would reveal ecstatic circumstances.

Win-win.

When we need to measure temperature, we use a thermometer as a gauge. I always made sure that my temperature before an appointment was peaceful, and I chose joy and expected excellent outcomes. My frequency had to be joy. I know it's hard, but again, the keyword is choice. And so we are clear, it didn't mean I had no fear, anxiety or discontent with the appointments. It just meant that I heavily leaned on my understanding of who God was, what He could do, and how He could use me in the situation. I kept faith that He would be there and step in for me when it would be too much. "Your threat means nothing to us. If you throw us in the fire, the God we serve can rescue us" (Daniel 3:16).

Appointments can feel heavy due to other people's opinions, energy, the obscene amount of information given, or the results you receive. Or maybe, you just really don't want to be there that particular day. Here's something I want you to remember in that room, on the car ride home, and when you have what I call "appointment hangover" for the next few days proceeding. What was said, the plan they made, the verdict that was said, the only option they said is available, is not the end. It's not. Nothing is happening that day. Nothing is entirely final. You were given information, which really is just information, and now you give it to God. You don't need to decide that second. Breathe, give yourself the grace to digest, do your due diligence, and make the right decision for you. I'm not saying that results or circumstances will always change or go exactly the way you're hoping for in the end. But, on that day, at that moment, in that appointment, know that that is just that day. Have hope and understanding that it is never too late for God. God has the final say, and He knows the best way. Not your way at the mercy of a situation or one professional opinion. Breathe, take in the information for what it is without denial, but don't you forfeit the match early and exit the ring. God is bigger. God is the last word. God changes things and can make the unexplainable happen in or out of an appointment. At that moment, hang on to hope and the promise He spoke to you.

Our Words And Our Thoughts

It can be the scariest yet most empowering realization when you genuinely understand your mind and mouth's power. I spent years starting to learn personal development before I got diagnosed- which in hindsight, was a portion of preparation God blessed me with. He always knows how to prepare you, even when you think you're not prepared.

However, I realized most of what I had learned didn't actually "click" until my C-word journey. I always read and heard over and over that "thoughts are things, focus on what you want, if you think and speak it, it will be." These are some things I'm sure you've also heard before. We take these things lightly when we don't want something bad enough, it doesn't hurt bad enough, or it's not life or death. We then wonder why our desired outcomes don't come when we casually think about it or spend a quick minute, focusing here or there. You need to become hyper-aware of your thoughts. Become a savage within your mind's battlefield, fighting for ground against the enemy, and opposition and negativity. You need to learn to become responsible for checking every thought passing through your mind. You are the only one in there.

Just you, no one else! Think about it. Until you become aware you have the power to alter your thoughts no matter how deep-rooted they are, you're going to believe your mind is running the show and that you're at the mercy of your sabotaging thoughts or self-limiting beliefs. Don't buy into this. You're learning to bob and weave, remember? You're quicker than that now. You control your mind. However, I am going to tell you that the process for perfecting this never ends because there should be no end. This process will be a constant, evolving, growing process for us because we are human. It takes intentional effort to master your mindset, give your thoughts to God, and rely on the Holy Spirit to provide you with the truth.

Every time you have a thought going through your mind, try saying, "And I'm happy it's that way." See if it's really something you want. If it's not, don't say it in your mind or from your mouth. And I know what you're thinking: "But Airam! The more I focus on not focusing on something, I focus on it more!" I get it, me too. I'm super complex up there. Are you ready for the secret? Until you can graduate to just saying, "next," at the moment negative thoughts come, focus instead on what you do want, not what you don't want. "I don't want the C-word" can turn into, "My body's healthy environment isn't an eligible host for the C-word to even thrive." See the difference? Because here's what's going to happen: What you think, you speak, and what you speak will shape the circumstance and physical reality you see around you and in you.

All your thoughts have shaped where you are right now. And you might be saying, "I wasn't thinking about cancer, losing my house, or job," or whatever the circumstance. You may not have been thinking about those exact things. Still, negative and trapped thoughts can manifest in our lives and body due to our emotions, past, trauma, and generational beliefs. And, even though we are here now, it can change. If you're overridden with blame, anger, or feel victimized, that won't help anything. Don't stay there. The goal is to strategize how to push forward and not get stuck in "why," remember? Look at it as the most empowering opportunity to now shape what's making it's way to you right now. We start together here and now.

Ask yourself tough questions. "Am I speaking life into my body and situation, or am I speaking death and negativity to the circumstance? Am I speaking hope and faith, or am I speaking fear and anger?" Suppose it is anything related to doubt, fear, timidity, lack, limitation, shame, anger, or loss of hope. In that case, it's not coming from God. God doesn't speak those things to you and God would never say those things about you or your circumstance. So, if it's not from God, it's a lie. It isn't the truth. It's a simple principle that can feel complex to apply at the moment, but if we keep it simple, it helps us move our minds in the right direction little by little. Practice and be gracious with yourself. Remember, you may be the only one in your mind, but you are not entirely alone. You are allowed, in fact, encouraged, to bring every thought to God. You have permission to ask Him, "Lord, is this of you? If it's not, I am placing it at your feet and I turn my trust to your truth. Please show me your truth." You have permission to say, "Lord, I am under attack with this thought or fear looping. I need help. You tell us you give us peace. I'm seeking peace." Your goal is never to be perfect in the mind but to have a perfect strategy. Being perfect in the mind isn't ever going to happen. Master your strategy.

Understand that you may not be fully able to have A+, constant, perfect, positive thoughts. You won't always be thinking you're blessed, steadfast, and that you trust God, and maybe, in a hidden moment, you question your faith or love for God. But, you can intentionally change your thoughts to God's thoughts and rewire your brain to create new patterns of thinking. New patterns can manifest God's will and your desires over your body and life. Being in alignment with truth is the natural state of our spirit. Not the fear and lack of knowledge that our ego works hard to depict. Remember when we earlier discussed begging versus declaring? I want you to understand you have the power to shape what's happening in your body and your situation. Seek God, seek His will, and then declare in relentless, affirming faith. Relentless.

Emotions And Energy

I'm a firm believer that trapped emotions within the body can manifest into disease, ailments, or sickness. Or, what some people call "dis-ease." It's important to remember that feelings are fleeting. One moment we are up, the next we can be down, to the left, or to the right. Our *feelings* aren't always reliable. *They are valid, but not always truthful.* This is why we come to prayer or ask God to give us an overpowering peace and wisdom over our emotions. I'm also a firm believer in energy, both what we put out and what we receive from other people or things. When going through the C-word, I viewed my body as a jar. That jar was getting filled no matter what. With what, was the question. It would either be filled with good emotion or bad emotion, good energy, or bad energy. I was cutthroat in protecting my body and spirit while going through the process. If something was good, I wanted it because I knew it wouldn't harm me but also would feed my spirit. If it was something bad, I didn't want it in or around me. It was a priority, and I mean top priority; the frequency of my body was healing and joy. I quickly realized whether my frequency was healing and joy, or not, stemmed from my thoughts, which stemmed from my emotions. And my emotions also impacted my thoughts. It's a cycle, really. The most important part of that realization was that I always had the simple but powerful choice of whether I wanted that jar to be filled with positive or negative. Again, knowing that it's going to be filled no matter what. I'd either choose or allow everything around me to choose.

Emotions are incredibly powerful. I view them as physical matter that take space in the body, like a light aura that takes on a shape and has movement. Negative emotions can manifest in external circumstances, aches, pains, and things you keep seeing occur in your life but can't figure out why, ailments, conditions, etc. I became hyper-intentional at examining the emotions I was feeling. Processing emotions is essential. It did not mean that I would not allow myself to feel normal negative emotions, but it did mean I wouldn't allow myself to stay there by choice. I needed to learn how to move gracefully through it like water and be aggressive in facing it head on to get to the root of the emotion. I needed to choose to refill the jar with more good constantly. Imagine you're holding an unending pitcher of water above your jar that's continuously flowing. Because the jar is full, it means water is also overflowing over the sides. If you have "bad" or "negative" in the jar and start pouring "good" and "positive" into it, the negative eventually overflows entirely out of the jar. When I would feel emotions like fear, anger or frustration, or someone else's energy weighing me down, I'd intentionally fill that jar with good through writing, a walk, meditation, essential oils, reading the Bible, and other avenues that worked for me.

My next point might be an unpopular opinion. And although I truly believe everyone has their own respected way of processing through something as fragile yet colossal as the C-word and understand it's different for everyone, this was my way. I sorted energy into only two categories and couldn't afford to gamble. I always saw it was widely popular for people to use hashtags, make apparel, or say out loud, "f**k cancer." *I get it.* I really do. It's a nasty, uninvited disease that no one wants, has taken far more lives of special people from other special people than we can comprehend, which, of course, makes us all hate this disease. I one hundred percent empathize and understand.

As someone who has been through it and has seen loved ones die because of it, I agree, but my approach was different. To me, saying F-you to the C-word was still saying F-you. Saying F-you resonates and feels rooted with anger and hate in my internal radar, even if intending to come from a positive place of triumph or empowerment. I needed to turn that same "passion" I had and use the same amount of energy to complete harmony and strength in my body. I found it contradictory to hate something inside my body and express resentment towards it while trying to heal the very same body at the same time. I find it impossible to keep my jar filled with positive and good while pouring fiery anger into it.

I did the exact opposite.

I'd talk to the C-word and thank it. "C-word, I understand that you temporarily need to be here in a physical sense for other people to see, but we both know you can't stay here. Thank you for giving me a platform for the biggest upset in my life. Thank you for being the vessel to show me how big and powerful God is. Thank you for being a lesson that is teaching me, stretching me, and preparing me for my purpose and growth. Thank you for being the very thing that will help me change the world. Thank you for being the thing that will allow me to help countless other people. I release you now." Gratitude and release. I believed God chose me. Yep, I thanked the C-word. You either think I'm a lunatic or you get it. I learned that in order to release the disease in theory, I needed to cover it in love.

Did you know that the way to conquer and release anything negative in life is love? Anger? Love. Fear? Love. Resentment? Love. Darkness? Love. To truly release is to love. So, I sent the emotion of love to the C-word. The frequency of my body, mind, and spirit needed to be love. It needed to be harmony, peace, and healing. I wasn't willing to compromise even if it meant doing what felt weird or what I didn't want to do at first. Believe me- deep down, I had the temptation to be angry at my body. It almost felt like a sense of betrayal that my body allowed this to happen. I felt anger, maybe even shame, that it didn't do its job to protect me. In any of our difficult trials in life, it's tempting and human to feel angry or bitter. But finding the gratitude and releasing what isn't serving you internally is a powerful antidote.

Don't turn against your body and give it rage and shame. Give yourself love. Give your body love. Give your body the same grace that Jesus gives us, and freely at that. Because what it opened my eyes to was the question, "How have I been betraying my own body?" Emotions are physical things that you cannot see in physical form. Still, you will see and are staring at them in manifestation in your body and life if you look close. You're carrying them every day, all the time, around the clock. Right now, I'm sure you have some emotions you've carried since before you can remember or maybe from trauma five years ago. You may be lugging around other people's emotions from boundaries you haven't learned to set, or perhaps from something that triggered you on social media earlier in the day. The list goes on. Truly understanding the impact of emotions on our health didn't come until about a year after I was C-word free. God was graciously exposing heavily rooted resentment, pain, anger, bitterness, and unresolved trauma from back in my childhood and adolescent life. My eyes were opened to how I re-created life scenarios with trapped emotions or unprocessed trauma, and how my body was holding these emotions. It was gracious that He led me piece by piece to find, make peace, and release these feelings, but it didn't mean that it was easy. Uprooting works the same way as the rest of the journey: the only way through is through.

I believe the Lord guided me to go inwardly to ensure that it would not come back. We can physically heal, but if we do not emotionally heal, I believe we aren't at the root. Again, it's a constant process. But my goal for you is to become aware of your emotional temperature. Ask yourself, "What am I feeling today? What am I feeling right now? Is my jar being filled with negative or positive? Where is this coming from?" The more you practice, the deeper you'll be able to go and resolve. Then, choose to find love towards these emotions and release. If you don't know where to start, start with God. He's always the safe bet to ask where you are in your emotions, and it's most reliable to bring those emotions to Him. You do not need to carry the weight of having all the answers to resolving your internal issues. Still, it is your responsibility to make yourself aware and proactive at dealing with them with the tools and grace God presents you with if you choose to be free from them. God wants freedom and peace in our spirits, too.

Victim vs. Victor

Being a victim versus victor is a fine line; be very careful. First, we need to be open to examining which role we are playing. Unintentionally, we can slip from being victorious to moving down the victim's rabbit trail without even noticing. When people found out I was going through the C-word, there was usually a sigh and a distinct look on their faces. They weren't doing it to make me feel bad; they were doing it to show sympathy, were overcome with concern which came from a good place, or didn't notice they were doing it. But 95% of the time, the proceeding words were, "I am so, so sorry." I kindly looked them dead in the eyes and asked them to please not be or say they're sorry. What came over me through God was that this would be God's victory over my life and that I didn't need sympathy; I needed faith. The words, "Don't take away my victory," usually proceeded humbly. They'd look at me like an alien, soften, and then look like, "wow."

It was powerfully apparent every time they felt a supernatural presence, that it was not me alone saying the words coming out of my mouth. We would both feel the presence. It was the Lord speaking through me to set a distinct stage for Him. Moments like this, you could just feel the air shift, and it's something you can only attribute to the Holy Spirit and angels and the spiritual realm meeting ours.

It became a personal slogan, and I invite you to have it be yours. I did not want people to feel sorry for me because the second they would feel sorry for me, I'd be tempted to feel sorry for myself and down the chute, I would go. People don't mean to do this, but they often project their responses based on how they would respond to the same circumstance as you. I know that the quick response was to feel sorry, but we feel sorry for someone's defeat. Not victory. Feeling sorry with pity and having empathy are two totally different things. So, I policed my environment and conversations. I had a one-track mind focusing on one thing only: Victory. And no one was going to take it away from me. Since God said it, it was my obligation to stay in line with the promise.

Your Body Is Your Temple

Your. Body. Is. Your. Temple. I'm inserting the clapping emoji between every word I just said. Friend, your body is your temple. "Don't you know that you yourselves are God's temple and that God's Spirit dwells in your midst?" (1 Corinthians 3:16). Your body is sacred and powerful. It's the holy home God sent your spirit to live in while here on Earth. It's the only one you get. It's the one who wakes you up every day, allows you to run and play, wondrously produces the miracle of life, breathes without you needing to think twice, detoxes to keep you alive, and works overtime to keep you safe. This body that you are in will fight to do the job that's needed to heal you the very best it can, and aiding it is going to maximize that. If the frequency we need to send the body is love, what are we saying to it when we intentionally don't care for it?

Anthony William, whom I absolutely love and highly suggest, says in his book *Cleanse To Heal,* "Just as someone who's been lucky for decades can come up against an exposure that leads to a health challenge at any age, so too can someone who has suffered health challenges change their fate. They key is to know how prevention and healing really work." I understand that not everyone's cancer is non-genetic, but this still counts even if they told you yours is. And, these same ideals count if you're reading this with no sickness at all. From plenty of learning, I discovered that genes can turn on and off. That's right. Even though the cancer I went through was non-genetic, my environment, myself, and my body created the perfect storm to precisely turn on specific genes that would allow that to happen. Some things I'm sure I did not have any say or intentional contribution to, and others, I'm sure I partook in some way or form.

In fact, remember how I mentioned that on my husband's side of the family, his grandma, grandma's sister, and mom all had breast cancer? Theirs was also non-genetic, yet somehow passed down from generation to the next. How does this happen? Habits, what we're exposed to, what we put in our bodies, and other factors. I was shocked and honestly disturbed that only about 10% of all cancers in the world are genetic. Ten, freaking, percent, of all cancer in the world that we see is genetic. I had my arms crossed, leaned back, with my gangster look on my face like, "Okay, game on."

I immediately said to myself, "If external factors had the power to create a perfect-storm environment in my body for this to happen, then dang-it, that means I also have the power to create an environment in my body where it can't live. I can at least try!" Game on. I'm not going to give you medical advice at what you should individually do here. Create your own plan, seek professionals and valuable information that resonate with you, learn about the body, foods, and exposure. However, I will give you brief insight as to what I did.

I cut everything out cold turkey that was going to inhibit health and healing, and fed my body an obscene amount of love through an overall wellness lifestyle. I made changes within my diet and added way more nutrients with wholesome organic foods, detoxed, limited processed food and sugars, educated myself on chemicals within food, worked to decrease inflammation in the body, used homemade remedies, chose fueling foods, herbs, and spices that would aid my specific case and so on. I researched optimal vitamin supplementation. I purged all the toxins out of my environment, home, and personal products. I didn't allow toxic fragrance, cigarette smoke near me, or alcohol in my body. I hydrated on the cellular level.

In terms of my outer body, exercise and sweating were important. I exercised regularly, probably five to six days a week, whether that meant going to the gym, going on a walk, or simple yoga and stretching. From a physical standpoint, this prepared my body for optimal healing for the surgery and supported my mental by giving me a positive outlet. The physical activity kept me sane most of the time. I genuinely believe it's why healing from my surgery was so expedited. I used to think of health as dieting earlier in my life. But what I have found is that it's not just about what foods or drinks to avoid; it's equally, if not more critical, to feed and fuel my body with what it needs for optimal performance, healing, and health. It's about learning how the body actually works. Learning about what causes disease. It's about being wholesome. I was going to give my body every freaking ounce of a shot I could give it because I may not be able to control the outcome, but I could control the effort and frequency of love and harmony in my body. It was inspiring for me to learn to love and respect my body in a whole new way.

I would give it what it needed to have the strength physically and mentally to go through the process. That also included: Wholesome sleep, eliminating stress, eliminating negative exposure (like violence in movies and music), and giving myself mental outlets. I imagined everything on a cellular level and these all played a part. Fueling my body was something I could help. If I had anything to do with it, I was relentlessly going to give my body everything it needed. One of my favorite books that was an excellent resource for me was How to Prevent and Treat Cancer with Natural Medicine by Michael T. Murray.

Obviously, this is a lot. I want you to be super careful here because it's really easy to create negative emotions and stress if this isn't done carefully. It's easy to blame yourself over and over again for the state of your health. But this isn't about blame, this is about empowerment. Looking at changing what you eat and thinking, "This sucks so bad I miss eating that," versus, "My body is being fed everything it needs to be a healing machine," is totally different. On the other hand, obsessively withholding from your body versus finding new healthy habits to provide nourishment is likewise detrimental. Looking at these lifestyle changes and feeling resentment, or trying to eliminate certain things but not replace them with nutritious items, will not do any good.

Think of starving the bad by replacing it with good. With that said, the word lifestyle is key. Think long term gain versus quick win even though this is an immediate need. Everyone is different in how they want to approach this: If you're okay going cold turkey and changing up your fridge in three days, then hallelujah. If it's better for you to slowly start replacing things here and there, changing portions, starting exercising by going on a 30min walk a couple of days a week, incorporating the extra hour of sleep you've been depriving, then that is also a hallelujah. Find solutions for you, but find solutions.

My point is that these changes are positive changes none the less, but make sure they are coming from the right place. Allow them to come from a place of wanting to heal and giving your body love, not stress. One thing I needed to practice was not to operate out of fear. It's incredibly easy, too easy, to go into overdrive that if you eat this or that, it's going make that thing grow, that you can never have this or that ever again. Habits start to become an unhealthy way of eating or not eating. No. No. No. I know that pressure and fine line all too well because I was there. I more so did this after the C-word where I would repeatedly say, "If I eat that, it's going to make it come back." It's just not the case.

First, by continually using the words, "make it come back," we are planting seeds in our influential minds that aren't the ones that work in our favor. Second, it is about mindfulness. Eating something one time absolutely will not make it come back. Operate at the soul level with your nutrition, so that it moves in harmony with your spirit. And, it's never a bad thing to ask for help! Remember, bob and weave—dance in the ring. Don't focus on what you don't want. Box back. Focus on what you do want. Instead of, "I can't and won't eat that because _____," move to, "I'm choosing to eat this because it's providing nourishment for my body." Focus on the gain, not the lack. I found nerdy excitement in researching what certain foods do for our bodies in and out of the C-word.

I loved picking foods from the market and combining foods knowing, "this is going to help this, this provides vitamins for that, that helps heal this, that helps fuel that." It became a way for me to make it fun, gave me hope, helped me be involved, excited, actively participating, and inspired.

Give your body the shot it deserves. Give your body love. Give it tools for healing. If you give it love, it will provide you with love in return. And let's not forget, your body includes your mind. We just went over emotions and energy, which ties into stress. Your stress and mental game are significant, and stress alone can be an authoritative source for all kinds of sickness. Take this seriously and make it a priority. My mom introduced me to essential oils, which I was skeptical about, but you try new things when your back is to the wall. I found that they dramatically helped me in acute situations to help me destress, relax and calm down. I also used them for immune support. There are amazing benefits you can look up, and it's all-natural. Also, take up meditation! It does not need to be complicated. I started by finding guided meditations on YouTube. I'd go on walks with healing sound frequency music or allow myself to nap or sleep with meditations. You can easily find these for free online, Spotify; you name it.

Starting somewhere is better than not starting, and incorporating a little is better than incorporating nothing. Remember that. If all these changes sound daunting, this is again, just what I did. One thing to remember is, at the end of the day, treating our body is a powerful tool and strategy. However, it is not the end all be all. God is. Don't put all your weight and pressure on being perfect with how you decide to approach your health. But make wise decisions. And friend, in case no one has told you today, you're doing great.

Outlets

You're going to need outlets that are productive towards the direction of your wellbeing and faith. Make time for these things! Figure out what type of activities help you destress, express yourself, put you in a happy place, and release anger, grief, or those challenging emotions: Journal, go to the gym, spend time outdoors, take up kickboxing or swimming, try meditation or yoga, have your most uplifting movies ready on your Apple TV cue, color or paint, listen to music, dance, read books; you get the idea. I'm not an advocate of just trying to find stuff to "keep you busy." Make your life busy with things that make you feel still. Fill it with things that make you feel alive. Huge difference. Having physical, emotional, and mental outlets will be so beneficial and necessary in your process because this journey creates a lot of stored energy within our body and mind. Remember, you need to do everything you can to enhance the good and release the bad from your jar. Give yourself opportunities to keep refilling! Be proactive about them and schedule them with as much importance as your time with family or appointments. Get that energy out, give yourself time to breathe, and channel on the right frequencies. And remember, just because we go through difficult times doesn't mean we don't have permission to laugh or feel joy while still in the middle of it. You are allowed to enjoy things, even amid a storm, and even if it's just for a moment or two.

Protect Your Mind

I want you to imagine your spirit and mind as your most valuable possession to protect. "More than anything you guard, protect your mind, for life flows from it." (Proverbs 4:23) Think of your mind and spirit as your baby. It is your responsibility to safeguard them with as much care and love as you possibly can. Sometimes this can be difficult, and might even feel selfish. I want you to think of your mind as the general, and your body as the army. The general's commands all operate from frequency, thoughts, and external influences. Whatever is being put into your mind will dictate your conscious and unconscious thoughts, which will then signal your army into action. What the mind says is what the body will follow.

You have no idea how powerful your mind is. The intricacy, capability, and amount of frequency that your mind sends to yourself and your external world is beyond your wildest imagination. "As someone thinks within himself, so he is." (Proverbs 23:7) If God is saying you have the power to create who you are, you also can create what's around you. I believe this is an open invitation to play with possibility. The way someone thinks within themselves determines what they are. If we are constantly saying, "I'm sick, I'm sick, I'm sick," or "I have this, I have this, I have this," then that is what will be, and that is what we will have. Don't miss this.

If you know that your mind has this amount of blatant, mystifying, and decreed power, why would you ever take arming and protecting it lightly? You have to have spiritual discernment for where you are getting council, who you vent to, what you turn to to make yourself feel better, and what you classify as fact. It might feel selfish or wrong to have to look at your mom or relative and know that they may be coming from a place of love, but that you cannot take their opinion. Sometimes, it's your close circle, could be acquaintances, and is what you watch, listen to, and read. You might need to discern the unsolicited advice that someone at church or your job gave you. But you need to focus on filtering what comes in because it will determine what gets put out. Remember, the general makes the calls, and the body is going to follow. Safeguard the general and never let your guard down. The Bible verse above tells you to protect. We only need to protect things that are under possible threat. The army and outcome of the battle depend on your strategy.

Power Of Prayer

Prayer changes everything. It is single-handedly the only thing that can produce change by the week, day, hour, and half hour. I've seen prayer move things by the minute. The thing with prayer is when we're new to practicing, it usually feels funny. It might start as forced time you allocate, or it might be a solid five minutes of silence because you don't know what to say, trying to formulate the "right" words to pray correctly. Sometimes, we are in such distress, confusion, or pain that we can't find any words. First off, God doesn't care about perfect sentence formulation, perfect verse memorization, or lack of structure when praying. He cares about your heart. He cares that you are seeking Him. He cares that you believe Him. He cares that you need Him. He cares that you're eager to see Him. He sees where you are, already knows what you're trying to say, and He hears you even when you feel like He doesn't. It is all about your heart. Second, because it's all about your heart, sometimes your tears and laying your heart out in silence to Him *is* prayer.

See, the miracles aren't going to happen because of your special prayer ability. God isn't looking for who the "best prayer warrior is." He will certainly use gifted prayer warriors. But it does not mean they are heard "more". He is looking for the man or woman that has faith. The willing vessel He can use. He is looking for those who have confidence in laying their heart down and giving it to God, daring to release their grip and giving the burden over and praising Him for His goodness even in chaos. They know He has the authority to respond and trust that. They know He hears them. Praying is not about just letting God know what our laundry list of needs and wants are, although He does deeply care. It's about connection. It's about worship, which is really just glorifying who He is in your heart. It's about seeking and going deeper and deeper to hear His voice. Praying is prioritizing God above ourselves. I mean this in a couple of ways: First, it's prioritizing that we know God holds the power, not us. Second, it's helping us move out of the way so that God can actually work.

When we pray, we are working in the spiritual realm. We're fighting our battles where it counts and where there is the power to afflict real change. The Bible shows us countless ways of how Jesus prayed and how He taught us all to pray. One thing that's important to note is that God answers prayers according to His will. How do you know what God's will is? You turn to the Bible to find what He says His will is. When you seek, you'll find it in plain text or other times in a parable. When my heart was ready to seek truthfully, I found answers to my own questions because I humbled myself to the fact that I may not like what I find but that it ultimately leads to my good. Then, bring your requests to Him and do your best to listen for His will in your situation. Not all prayers get answered in the way you want or expect, but they are heard. If it's not the exact way you wanted it to be answered, trust me, it's a really good plot twist for more of whatever it is you're truly asking for. It's important to understand you're not always going to love the answer you get or that it's going to be a yes. However, if it wasn't a yes, He has a different plan that's bigger and better. Stay extremely firm in faith that He works for your good and always has your best interest. If you can always start there, you're starting in the right place.

I believe that God hears our prayers, even more, when we recruit other people to pray with and for us. The Bible tells us that when two people come together in agreement on anything at all and make a prayer of it, God moves into action. And when two or three of us are together because of Him, seeking Him, we can be confident He is there with us (Matthew 18:20). Remember, even though I didn't tell very many people until later in the journey, I was praying fervently with the few that knew and little by little asked people to join us. You do what feels right for you and how you're guided. In my experience, the act of asking someone to pray for me alone has been a signal of devotion to God. It is an act of stepping out, which moves the heavens into action. What I found was power on two spectrums.

First, I wanted to recruit people who were fully aware of their authority in prayer and would powerfully intercede, believe, and declare with me. I wanted prayer warriors on the battleground with me that I knew would graciously give their hearts to fight the battle with me in the spiritual realm (*I can never thank them enough*). This is the most valuable, sincerest gift I believe we can give someone, by the way. Second, I kindly asked or mentioned praying to people who didn't have the most powerful prayer lives. In fact, I very well knew some, if not most people, didn't pray at all. But tragedy, illness, or fear tend to lead people to God, a heart seeking to believe in something or softens their hearts to pray. I prayed that if I humbly asked some of those people to pray, that maybe they would, and then they would see God's miracle through me and have even a grain of belief that He is real. I honestly believed that if there was a person who said a prayer for me, calling out on my behalf, who had never prayed or fully believed in God, that that was more of a win than those who prayed regularly.

My foundation for prayer is always to do and honor what would be most pleasing to God, for His glory to be shown in whatever facet that is. Not only does God want to see where your heart is while praying, but He wants the opportunity for Him to be seen through the miracle. He wants others to see your devotion to praying. By the time the hundreds of people knew what I was going through on the day of my surgery, I believed with all my might that every person's prayer counted, and they did. When I won, they won. We need people to stand in the gap for us when we don't have the strength. God finds it pleasing when we ask others for prayer and lay our hearts down for others in their needs.

Minute-To-Minute-Basis Practice

While going through difficult seasons, there will be some moments you'll be on a high of faith, a peak of joy and appreciation, and get waves of positivity. Other times, you're going to feel fear, spikes of anger, anxiety, and confusion. Remember that turning to Christ does not make you superhuman. But it does give you superhuman access to the One who can supernaturally change your circumstance. We need to grow to be extremely intentional with what I call, SSA: Spiritual Self Awareness. SSA is asking yourself, "Where am I spiritually? Am I engaged? Have I drifted? Am I distracted? Is my spirit thirsty? Do I have any clue where my spirit is? Do I even feel my spirit?"

Why? Because I found that when we're not in survival mode, we're pretty much on autopilot. I became so conscious of this when going through the C-word. There are so many thoughts and emotions flying around at once. The funny thing is that this is happening when we're in survival mode or not. We just hear it more resoundingly and loud when we're in a steady state of panic, crisis, and fight or flight. See, most of the time, when things are "fine," we don't have a reason to be intently listening to every thought every minute. The thoughts are quieter overall, not in heightened states, and you're on cruise control. We aren't in constant defense or distress, hyper-vigilant about examining our surroundings, protecting ourselves, or in fight or flight like a bear is about to attack us.

When we are in survival mode, the thoughts instead bombard us without us seeking them and in fact, without a care for our permission. It feels like we can't stop them, and they overtake us, sometimes paralyzing us in the overwhelm. The devil loves this. He loves the unrest, the rabbit trails, and the looping because it's easy for him to weasel his way into confusing you as to whom the thoughts belong to. Normally, days just seem to pass, and although filled with exciting and good things, we go about our routines with more ease and minutes merge to hours, hours merge in the day. We must strategize for the autopilot to still be optimal. The Bible tells us never to let our guard down and to "be alert...Your enemy, the devil, prowls around like a roaring lion looking for someone to devour" (1 Peter 5:8).

What I learned was to take things literally by the moment. Sometimes that was by the hour, but a lot of the time, it was literally by the minute. Sometimes by every 30 seconds or down to the second. I became so acutely aware of my thoughts, in some ways by choice, in many other ways not, because it was my only option. The Bible tells us to take every thought captive (2 Corinthians 10:5). Your mind is a battlefield, and there is warfare you cannot see. There is a war for your mind and the enemy knows the power that lies within there for your healing, wellbeing, peace, joy, and access to your ultimate source: God. It's going to be attacked, point-blank.

When wars happen, each side doesn't go into battle blind-sighted without a strategy. When someone wages war on a country, they don't just "hope" the enemy doesn't overtake and win. They protect, they guard, and they fight. They don't only "hope" that the enemy doesn't attack. They plan for it. They have an action plan, a defensive and offensive strategy. This has to be you. This was me. This continues to be me. Here is a strategy for you that I used. First, you need to be heavily filled with the Word. The Bible is your sword (Ephesians 6:16-18). This is your truth that is the secret weapon to defeating your opponents. It's what you will stand on when your thoughts are waging war and starting to overtake that halfway point of gaining ground. This is how you gain your ground back. This is your peace. This is your strength. This is your truth when you don't understand what's happening or where you're going, and everything you see and hear is contradictory to the promise you heard.

Write down the thoughts you are continually having (*yes, they can be scary to look at on paper*). Then, I want you to open up that Bible, your sword of truth, and start reading your way through it and allow it to breathe into you. Wherever you start or land on is okay. Maybe you just start where there is a verse that speaks to you. Read through the story and see what it's working on within you and the perspective it's trying to show you. Learn how Jesus moved in that passage. Let it work in you and speak to you. What proof in the Bible has been displayed for conquering this thought or this instance? Remember, if the feelings attached to your thoughts are anxiety, fear, panic, confusion, or loss of hope, it's not coming from God. Pick up your tool and seek the truth of what God says.

It brings me the most unfailing calm to know that because it is the truth, and God is almighty, it has more authority than my own thoughts and feelings or the enemy's whispers.

What does the Bible say for how you feel? What about what you're going through? Use this as your basis for your thoughts. If it says it, it is. And the comforting thing that you will find is that with Jesus, it always leads to victory. Have confidence and peace because there is an answer in there for you; no matter what you are facing, what you are feeling, or what you are thinking, I promise it's there. Jesus either felt it, experienced it in a parallel manner, or has set the path through stories of people just like you and me; humans who were flawed and in need of help and direction.

The Bible is a living, breathing mirror to your life, trust me. And something I want to point out is that if you say, "well, we don't sacrifice animals or have the same laws," you're missing the point. Dig deeper. Sit longer. Move out of the literal, and move into the spiritual context. Dwell and explore. I want you to keep the Bible truths that speak to you with you until they are muscle memory. Every time a thought invades, look at that truth and repeat that in your mind until it takes ground back. Declare it. Put your foot down. Shake it off and lay the punch. At first, it's going to feel funny and maybe even useless. It'll feel like you're saying it without believing it or not being heard or answered. It's going to take practice to drown out the noise. It will take patience to believe God is working behind the scenes and seeing it through. And, a secret is that the noise will never stop. You will just become excellent at nipping it faster and filling yourself with the truth versus suffering in the lie.

You'll become an assassin at quickly disarming the opponent in your mind. Keep repeating it while humbly asking God to give you His truth because you believe it is the truth even if you don't feel it yet. Even if you don't see it yet. Do this on a minute to minute basis. Next, pick mantras. Some of mine were, "Every single cell in my body is healthy. My body is in perfect harmony. My body is on a frequency of love and health." For those of you not going through a health crisis, it could be that you are declaring for your finances to change, for the Lord to save your marriage, for your children to come to the Lord, that dream to come alive, for God to intervene in a deeply troubled circumstance, or to be free from guilt or shame of the past. Build your own strategy. When the thoughts come in, when the doubt creeps, when something triggers you, your chest starts to rise in overwhelm, the lump in your throat starts to form, and it physically feels like you can't escape your mind, you put your gloves up, and you strike. These are the moments when you're collapsed on the floor or pulled over on the side of the road. You say, "enough." You use your ammunition. You fight. And you win.

Minute to minute basis also applies to joy. Yes! Joy. When going through the C-word, I wanted to feel joy all the time. And, maybe in part, because I was terrified not to feel joy. I desperately wanted relief and to be hopeful. I wanted to feel the weight off my chest, smile, and feel pain in my stomach from laughing because what was my alternative? More than anything else I heard from people over and over, they always told me I was so full of joy and positivity in the process. And you know what? I'm proud of that. I knew I was supernaturally full of joy. But, you need to know that I did not just "wake up like that." I worked to feel joy, and joy is what I genuinely got. I got what I earnestly worked to project so that I would get it in return. I quickly realized the actuality that I wasn't just going to "feel" happy without making conscious choices to get there and some drill work or "training" to rewire. I wasn't just going to "have" joy while it felt like my world was shaking underneath me. I wanted to crawl into a ball, had so many questions, and every step felt like taking a beating some days. I needed to work for that joy in the waiting and stillness. It took focus when all I wanted was to be physically told it would all be okay to confirm what I believed and what my spirit knew, but no one could do that. Joy had to be a choice on a minute to minute basis.

It was a pre-meditated but, at times, incredibly uphill and painful choice. Some days I flat out didn't want to have to make the choice. But I made it, and you can too. Even when there were days I was upset with God, moments I wanted to scream or was in fetal position, times I publicly cried on the treadmill at the gym or when my journal writing was angry scribbles that lead to rips on the page, I chose to choose joy. What does it mean to choose joy? That you make yourself feel better? No. It means you remember that one of Jesus' willing sacrifices was to give you peace that surpasses all understanding (Philippians 4:7). What does this mean? That the peace doesn't need to make sense to us or be logical in this world. But you have to choose to seek by coming to Him, who will freely give it to you. The choice you make when you want joy is to choose Him. I'd tell myself it's okay to be where I was for that moment, but that it's time to ask God to hold my hand to get up. It's time to take a step. It's time to re-focus. Breathe, roll my shoulders back, close my eyes, fill my jar with good, and ask God to supernaturally take over when I needed Him. But make a choice. You do this over and over and over again until peace leads to joy. When you choose to place your joy in the hands of God, it is sustainable not situational.

Making Decisions

One of the most challenging things I encountered when going through this process was making decisions for my trajectory. Remember, I was only 27. Not that it's easy at any age to stand up to the medical world, but I felt a few of the doctors that came in my path saw my age as subordinate. As if I couldn't possibly have any clue at what would be best and that I was too young to understand. I had a few instances where I was bullied for my beliefs of combining holistic health with western medicine. I was told that I may be irrational for my faith and that if I didn't fall in line with what they were suggesting, it would be my fault if treatment wasn't successful now or in the future. One thing I tell everyone as an important disclaimer is that everyone's trajectory is entirely different. What worked for me may not work for you, what happened to me may not happen the same to you, and what worked for someone else wasn't what worked for me but worked for them. My miracle might not be yours, and someone else's wasn't mine. However, I believe you don't need to be silent in your care.

Sometimes, we move to give God the big things, that we forget that He also moves in the small things; the "in-between" and practical items. We forget that we can pray about the more minor parts of the overall situation. Making decisions in your journey is difficult because the pressure is on you; the outcome is dependent on the choice you make. In a case where the decisions could mean life or death and have a significant impact on the trajectory of your life, the pressure can feel crushing. Some things you can't go back on- like removing a whole breast, but others have more flexibility, if you will, such as stopping medication after trying it for a little while. But, just as Hezekiah did with the threatening letters from his enemies, you can do the same with all the details. He "went to the Lord's temple. He spread them out in front of the Lord and prayed to the Lord" (2 Kings 19:14-15).

Bring every detail to Him. Lay every option and every honest thought attached to it at His feet. My sister-in-law once told me that talking to God is like a radio frequency. God is not the author of confusion but gives us clarity, soundness, and peace. Sometimes, however, it takes a lot of pressing and patience. Sometimes, God is working by being silent and not giving you the exact answers right off the bat for your decisions. He is stretching your capacity to lean in. Think of it as Marco Polo. He inches himself further and further to test our faith and push us to our victories. It's the enemy's job to distract you. He loves to torture you in your mind, cause turmoil, fear, and doubt of yourself, God, and your promises God gave you. Back to the radio frequency; to hear the song's sound, you have to keep fine-tuning through the static. Suppose you are not on the right frequency. In that case, you're picking up voices and sounds from other stations or just getting obnoxiously loud radio noise. You need to press in through the noise and patiently keep seeking His voice's sweet sound. Peace.

The pressure can really stack with some decisions. My most challenging moments were standing up to experienced doctors pushing me to do rounds of chemotherapy, radiation, and removing both of my breasts. The other incredibly hard decision I struggled with was hormonal therapy pills after the C-word was done. You're going to have to make burdensome decisions in your journey that feel intimidating. But guess what? God knows that you are only human. He knows you can't bear it on your own and offers help. If you lay it all at His feet, drop off the load He's encouraging you to hand over, and listen for that song He has just for you, you will be guided to the right place. He will have you meet people with expert knowledge for what you specifically need, or maybe lead you to an article or book that reveals an answer. He can provide tools, resources, or alternatives, and options you never thought of. He will open doors and shut others. He will nudge and encourage, strengthen you to stand "surefooted as a deer, enabling (you) to stand on mountain heights" (Psalm 18:33) when you need to face opposition, and give you a comforting embrace when you feel all alone. Give Him every single tiny detail. They are safe with Him.

Hearing What You Hear But Not In Denial

Do you know how many times we hear the word "no" before we are even five years old? I've read studies that mention, as toddlers, we hear the word no over 200 times a day. A day! It shows how we are conditioned when we get told no, to conform to a certain degree. The same goes for when we hear something and submit to its validity that it's the "end," the final say, or the last word. I've encountered a few major moments in my life when I distinctively heard God say, "I understand you hear what you're hearing, and I know you see what you're seeing, but I need you to trust me."

Have you ever died from a no? No. Is it the doctor verbally telling the patient that they are now diagnosed with something that physically kills the person? No. I don't believe that circumstances, what we see, or what we hear are the last words or the final act. I believe it's never over until God says it's over. It's not the whole picture. And not one of those things is bigger than God. Period. When I first got that call telling me that it was the C-word, it was very distinct that it wasn't the final say. There was more to this story. There was something God was doing that was surpassing what I heard. I never once believed the C-word was something I had. It was something I was going through for a much larger purpose. I never spoke, thought, or believed I was sick. This didn't mean that I was in denial; it meant there was more to the story. I didn't deny the diagnosis. But I wasn't going to deny what I knew about God and what He does, either. I understand you may be looking around saying, "There's no way." Do you know how many reluctant prophets were looking around confused or afraid of the assignment God gave them or the calling placed in front of them that looked disastrous or crazy?

When life smacks you in the face and knocks you to your knees, it's not about being in denial of the situation. It's not putting your head in the sand and burying the fact that the situation exists. But, why it exists, and the "from above perspective" versus the "here and now" perspective are more critical things to look for. I heard what they were saying when they gave the diagnosis, when the doctors told me the lump size was more than double what they initially thought it was, and when they gave me every figure and statistic to justify their treatment recommendations. I didn't deny that those things were real and factual, but my perception was that those were only one piece to the puzzle. The more opposition in what I saw or heard, I'd say to myself, "Man, this miracle will be big. But it's not too big for Him." The matter of the miracle happening never wavered, but the "how," I left up to God. It's about getting up and choosing faith regardless of the facts because you believe. It's about understanding that you are not limited to what you see or hear with God because you believe the spiritual realm uncovers the truth of the situation. It's about pivoting your stance and turning to the Father to ask for understanding. This type of faith comes from a humble yet unshakeable place of surrender. We don't go around telling people they're wrong or that the facts aren't true. Instead, we stand firm within what we know through Him.

Feeling Alone

When I first got diagnosed, I went into silent assassin mode. It was like a Nintendo gear got turned all the way up. Even though God was speaking loud and clear to me, sometimes, it still felt lonely. In both our flesh and spirit, the only person who can genuinely, one thousand percent, hear God in our situation is ourselves. The Lord will send divine people in our path to pray with us and for us. He might use them as tools to speak His wisdom, but they still will not fully hear God in your situation to the extent that He is directly trying to speak to you about it. Even though you have God and know you're not alone, sometimes it still feels lonely because you're called to walk in a trench that no one else will fully understand. Nor are they able to walk it with you.

You know it's you that has to walk through, and it's a journey intended between you and God. You've heard what God is doing, but no one else has. I've related to the phrase, "You don't get it," many times. We all have. But this was a whole different beast. I furthermore understand that even though you may have the full, loving, intentional, and evident support of a spouse, family, and friends, it may still feel alone because none of them have been where you are. In your exact shoes. In my case, I was fortunate that I at least had my mother-in-law and grandma-in-law that had been through it before to compare logistics and share our belief in God. I had the most supportive, loving, selfless, cheering, and listening husband. I had praying and encouraging best friends that believed with me and would help talk me off the ledge when I needed it. But even then, I still remember feeling alone because it was just me in the trench.

Alone that I was only 27 at the time, and I didn't know a single person I could talk to that had ever been diagnosed with breast cancer at the same age. I remember I knew maybe two other people in my relative circle around my age that had been through any kind of cancer at all. I was desperate just to feel some sort of connection, some kind of understanding of what I was going through emotionally and physically. I was desperate to find proof in someone that I was going to be okay. But I quickly learned that what God was doing in me wasn't something typical I would find. It was going to have to be me to walk in the trench so that when others got there, they would know it could be done.

Some people encouraged me to join breast cancer support groups at the hospital. I gracefully said no, thank you. No one would be around my age, and I didn't want to force myself to go to the hospital more than I needed to if it didn't feel it would serve me. I didn't want to place myself around other people with any chance they would innocently call themselves or me sick- according to this world, that's what cancer is single-handedly classified. I was afraid to be around other people that wouldn't have the same belief as me for what I knew about my trajectory. Even though we on paper were on the same path physically, I knew where I was spiritually, and something told me this wasn't the place for me to be. It was not at all that I thought I was better, that they were wrong, that I didn't empathize with them, or that they wouldn't have anything to contribute to my wellbeing. I'm sure there would be some things I could find in common and even take away. But there was an intense focus I had that I wasn't willing to compromise. In that moment, it's what was best for me.

I wasn't willing to risk it. One time, I went on a forum online and never went back on again. Again, I one hundred and fifty percent respect and know that everyone has their process and what will work for some won't work for others. If you find comfort and help in online forums or support groups in your process, that's amazing and encouraged. I sincerely mean that. If you don't, that's also okay. In my case, I stayed distanced. See, because of feeling alone in the process, I thought that maybe if I went online and found some groups where people would talk about their experience, I would find community or comfort.

The problem was that when I went on these forums for answers, a sense of someone knowing how I felt, or finding a similar experience, I didn't like reading about how they felt or what they went through at all. It not only didn't help me find what I was looking for, but it also made me feel extraordinarily negative and out of focus. It was a distraction. I started searching for a few answers here and there. Truthfully, what I found in the support groups were women finding community in the pain, struggle, negative side effects, and being trapped by the same cookie-cutter treatment trajectory that we all got from a doctor. Every one of us. My truth is that by reading into other people's scenarios, discouragements, what happened to them, and asking if there was "anyone else experiencing" blank, I felt discouraged. When normally, sharing commonalities would help us feel understood, I felt myself losing hope.

I felt the energy coming through every word I read rooted in anger, resentment, and fear. I found myself comparing my health trajectory to theirs, which slyly tried to instill in me what would or wouldn't be possible based on their results, what their doctors said, what their bodies felt, what worked for them and what didn't, and what they believed possible. They weren't me; what God was doing in me is not what God was doing in them and vise versa. This awakening taught me a powerful parallel lesson in comparing life trajectories with other people. What God is doing in and for you is for you and you alone. It's impossible to truly compare with others because I don't believe in this Earth's limitations. God may use similar trials or arenas, but what He is doing in you and what He's doing it for is different than anyone else's trajectory. Because it didn't happen for other people doesn't make it impossible for you. God is doing something intricate in you, right here, right now that is tailored to just you.

When I sat in my bed, literally sobbing reading a lot of the answers and opinions I thought I was looking for, what stood out to me was God whispering to me,

"Do you want these results?"

I whispered, "No," in timid, defeated fear.

"Then why are you searching here," He asked?

"Where do you see me in this?

Who is the more trustworthy and loyal reference?"

I remember, at this point, I was lying on my side in my bed in the middle of the late morning, crying with my hands grasping my pillow over the top of my head and my ears. Without me needing to say it out loud, my spirit knew that I didn't hear Him in those other people's experiences. I didn't see or feel Him in it at all. Not to say He wasn't there for them or working in them and through them. But where I was seeking answers and validation wasn't the place He wanted me to pursue. I wasn't going to find any answers there for me.

Sometimes, we vent or seek advice from the wrong place and the wrong people. It doesn't make those places or people bad. It just makes it not the right place and opens a door for the enemy, and this is an important place to have discernment. The enemy also knows you're seeking information and answers. We can be tricked into thinking we are finding council in the right place. Be careful where you vent, and be cautious about where you get fed.

God was protecting and nudging me, encouraging me with patience, like when we watch a child try to figure something out without giving them the answer right away. He was embracing me like the loving parent He is. He knew where I was coming from and knew my intention was just to feel not alone. He knew I was honestly looking for answers and that I was innocently trying to piece together the trauma of what was happening in my world. And, I knew it hurt Him, watching me break as I imagine it would for any loving parent.

Truly, the thought of my future child hurting and going through the trials and fire I know they need to go through will be tough for me. As parents, there are some things they can't just swoop in and "fix" for their kids; at least they shouldn't. We know it's a process they have to go through to grow for their good. They have to derive at the destination on their own, but it's a parent's job to guide. God works this way. In the same sense, although I am in your corner, although I am coaching you, although I am jabbing and punching with you as if I was the one fighting and calculating the strikes with you, you are the one in the ring. I can't fight for you, and neither can anyone else—just you. The only way through is through. So, find support where you need it. But be mindful of whether the help is distracting you from your victory or empowering you towards your desired outcome.

I'm not coaching from the textbook. I'm coaching from experience. But far beyond, and incomparably more of a model than I am, Jesus is the ultimate teacher and link to wisdom. I promise you He knows what you're going through and how you feel. Your pain pains Him. It's displayed in the Bible that He wept and was even angry when Lazarus died

(John 11:33-35), or in Psalms when He gets so furious at enemies attacking David that He comes down in wrath (Psalm 18:7-13). So even though He is almighty powerful and supernatural, He still feels for us and with us, the way you and I humanly feel.

Probably times a million.

I believe that sometimes, a considerable part of the alone factor isn't even that we're searching for someone to relate by having the same kind of C-word we had. It's not that we're looking for someone going through EXACTLY what we're going through in life. It's more so that we feel alone because we believe that no one could possibly know how we feel to the fullest extent. Other people may have gone through what we have gone through, or know someone who has or have valuable life experience from their own life. It does help, but sometimes, "It's not exactly the same," we say. This is how we feel, at least, isn't it? What I've learned is, we're right.

Others won't always know exactly how you feel, and it's not the same, even if maybe they have gone through exactly what we're going through. You know why? Because they're not us and we're not them. It's good to invite people in, allow other people to relate and help, and do the same vise versa. Still, it's impossible to know exactly how each other feels to fill that empty space we desperately seek to fill completely. In fact, it's unrealistic and setting ourselves up for disappointment to try to find someone that can understand our exact pain and emotions to truly make us feel not alone through and through, without fail, all the time, and nail it right on the head. There are spaces in us that other people cannot fill. God did this on purpose. We instead need to know that people are with us, that they understand and care to understand.

But I have good news. There is someone who does know exactly how you feel, through and through. Jesus. He knows my sweet friend. He supernaturally knows every fiber of your heart, thoughts, and feelings because He beats as one in you and with you. He feels for you and with you on a level that we physically can't comprehend because we don't have that capability. My heart is breaking with you because I can imagine what you have felt or are currently feeling. But even I don't know exactly what you're going through, and collectively, exactly how you feel. Because our minds are different, our past traumas are different, our life experiences have been different, our specific cases are different, how we are wired is different, our support system is different, our willingness to not face defeat is different, our faiths are different- We are different.

We are human. And I know in this life, it can feel devastatingly alone sometimes. But you aren't. You are not alone. If you don't have one person in your life that sees you, I see you. If you don't have one person in your life, know that I am with you, although it may not be physically. If you feel like you have no one, know that I pray for you. I do. If you don't have one person that understands or cares to see what you're going through, I do. I'm in your corner in the ring. Right now, I am with everything I have, transferring strength to you. But, even more comforting, let me get out of the way and point to the source, the only source, who can fill that void of loneliness that no one on this planet can fully fill. When you hear the whisper that knows that you have people who love and support you, but it can feel like they don't really know, Jesus knows. He sees you. He's with you in that dark trench. Visualize me in your corner. I want you to try one more thing:

I want you to close your eyes. I want you to envision yourself in the boxing ring. You're in the world's largest arena, and every seat is filled, not one open. I want you to look up and see the screen that is lining the perimeter of the arena that has words passing by. It says your name circling the arena. I want you to feel the heat of the lights penetrating that ring and be blinded looking into them. It's so bright in the ring, and dark out there, that you can't see the crowd. You can only hear them. Feel your current fears as you stand there. Feel your pain. Heck, even feel your anger. Feel it. Feel it right now in your physical state. Don't run from it inside. Your eyes are still closed. I want you to look at your opponent. Whatever you see your opponent as, it's in the "person" stepping side to side, punching their gloves together, staring at you with a hellish smile. Feel your fear. Now I want you to imagine the crowd disappearing. You feel an overwhelming presence coming from behind you that at first frightens you by its authority without looking behind you. It's the presence of God. There is radiating, bright light. And although His stature is peaceful, His presence is fearfully powerful. He is staring at your opponent, and you notice that your opponent's cocky mannerisms start to change. The opponent stops swaying, the smirk is gone, and they're at a standstill with a look of growing intimidation on their face. You soon realize that it's not you that's changing the stature of your opponent. You turn around, and instead of looking eye to eye with Jesus, you slowly have to look up because His presence and stature fill the space all the way to the top of the arena. His beaming light is stretching from the very left of your side of the arena, all the way to the very right, blinding the entire opposing side. He's not saying anything, and His expression hasn't changed, He just IS in His powerful presence. Jesus looks down at you and calmly signals you to look at your hands with His eyes. There is light that is fast-moving like an electric aura around them. The more you look to His size, the aura grows brighter and starts to build in energy. The more you believe, your internal fear disappears. The intimidation and anger have channeled into God's power. You realize that your hands are filled with His power. You are filled with His power, He is within you, and you within Him. You are not alone.

Handling Relationships While Going Through This

Relationships are such a complicated factor when going through this process or any major trauma. I know. I sometimes still cry, thinking back on the pain and fear I felt when going through the C-word being newly married to my husband. It's gut-wrenching. I've learned that I'm relentlessly fierce when I need to put my suit on and plow through. But that's precisely what I do. I plow ruthlessly, and I will not let down. I'm determined. When I was diagnosed, my first thought was my husband, which I shared with you before. Then, I thought about my mom. For you it might be your spouse, it might be a parent, it might be your children, it might be your very best friend, or maybe the people you are leading with your life's passion. It's whoever is occupying that intense and mysterious space of love and purpose in your being.

I know the slow-motion realization when the punch gets laid. I know the movie-like slow-moving picture of their face coming to your mind and piercing your heart. Your heart breaks at the shadow of a possibility of being without them, but part of you also breaks at the thought of them being without you. "It wasn't supposed to be like this," comes to mind. I understand the racing fear and the animalistic scream you want to let out. I know the sheer pain. Because let's face it- Cancer is scary. And it quickly puts losing or being without our loved ones into an authentic scenario that you wouldn't otherwise experience. Going through the C-word taught me the expression, "I love you so much it hurts." I also understand that you love that person or those people so unbelievably much that you refuse to show weakness. I never wanted to show fear to my husband or my mom. To anyone, really.

I know the feeling of being terrified to show any sign of fear, halfway because you don't want them to worry or be afraid, and you're protecting them. Halfway because if you see them break down, you'll break down. So, you lead. And if you're like me- you plow. Viciously. And while it's the bravest thing to do, I know the turmoil going on inside. I understand the teeter-totter of deeply needing their love and support, while unintentionally pushing them away because in secret, or not so secret, you're just trying to breathe above water while violently drowning at the same time. And, you're partway afraid and preparing to ease yourself into the idea of dealing with the morbid reality of sickness, the unknown, and afraid to hold on to the life you love with them so deeply. See, the tough thing when going through significant blows is that life is still happening. Life is always moving around you, and it can be challenging to manage because everything has changed and stopped in your world. In my case, I felt like I took up an intense calling that required my full attention and energy. Although I know better from a healthier standpoint now, I felt entirely responsible and carried enormous weight. I became obsessed and focused and felt I didn't have a choice.

While this was what I felt I needed to do, this had natural repercussions. There was significant sacrifice I went through and saw that sometimes it wasn't understood. I always mention to people that it wasn't just me who went through the C-word. Mikey and I did. We went through it together in our way as a union. It may have been me walking in the trench, but I understand he had one of his own. I respect him tremendously for his and am forever grateful for his sacrifice. I know you relate to this based on whomever that person or those people are in your life. It quickly changes dynamics, circumstances, and roles before you can prepare. There is no choice. You're thrown into the ring with no warm-up and in pure survival mode. That's tough. In our case, we had only been married a year and a half and never expected this at all, let alone at our ages. I always believed God paired Mikey and me together as an orchestrated dynamic of grit, grace, strength, and power. Others saw that as well from the start of our relationship. But as strong as we were, it was also still very challenging. We're tough, but we're human. Here is the basis of what I want you to understand, remind yourself, and remind your village:

You are on the same team.

You are all scared, but you are on the same team. As difficult as things may get, the enemy is not anyone or anything else. The enemy is only the enemy using circumstances. We are all doing the best we can, with where we are, what we know, and what we've got. You are doing the very best you can. They are doing the very best they can. But you are on the same team. Can I say that again? I need you to understand that I know you didn't ask for the C-word to come to your doorstep. But I also need you to remember, the other people in your life didn't ask for this either. They are coping just as much as you are in their own way, adjusting and trying.

In hindsight, it is clear as day that my husband and I went into pure survival mode. I did what I thought would be best to survive, and so did he. I did the best I could to stay around for him, and he did the best he could to help me do what I needed to survive. Sometimes that powerfully merged and aligned with our special bond and other times that caused a rift.

I know that your relationship dynamics are changing. I know that you guys have a new routine. I know that finances and responsibilities are coming into play. Sacrifices are made. I respect my husband tremendously and admire that he worked so hard to make sure we would be good financially and gave me the space to just focus on my health. But, not everyone has this privilege. I also am familiar with emotions fluctuating in such a fragile and scary time. Intimacy transforms. You're trying to be as "normal" together as possible. Simultaneously, there's a massive elephant in the room that you're both terrified because you love each other so much. The way you interact with each other isn't the same because sometimes it's overly in love, and other times it's based out of fear. Your focus and energy aren't the same. You aren't crazy, and you aren't alone. You are human, and from the words of one of my friends, "You're doin' it. And you're doing great." Things appear different from different perspectives. Please learn from my experience that this is so incredibly important to practice grace and understanding here. Let me give you an example.

When I got diagnosed, I quickly went into "clean sweep" mode. I drastically changed my diet, stopped drinking any alcohol, and cleaned out every toxic product in our house. I didn't ask for permission to do this. I just did and without question, because I took charge of my health. Repercussions for this were that my husband and I's regular eating habits no longer matched at all; we barely ate out anymore because I was so strict about what I put in my body, and not that our lives were only centered around drinking, but it was part of our norm to have drinks here and there socially. Us going out became almost nonexistent because if I wasn't going to drink,

I didn't want to be around it. I wasn't in the mood to be "on the scene." And again, everyone around us was incredibly supportive of me, but it was me excluding myself being so focused on being focused; Survival mode. What impact do you think this had? My husband justifiably felt this was maybe obsessive, unfair, "cold turkey" and a drastic lifestyle change he had no say in. It had a significant impact on the social life and community he needed to destress from his survival mode and created an environment of shelter and guilt.

My husband thrives off of being autonomous and social. He's the light of the room. We both always have been very social, outgoing, fun, thriving people. This was a drastic and immediate change he didn't plan on or ask for from a person that felt entirely new. Granted, because my husband loves me and wanted me to be in the best possible space he could provide, he without question was incredibly graceful, caring, patient, and willingly partook in the changes. Of course, he also wanted me to be here, so he did the best he could to let me do what I needed to do. But, what happens when we have to repeatedly sacrifice ourselves for others sometimes? Resentment may form under the surface. How do you think this affected him in the immediate and long term? Now let's look at it from my perspective.

I was angry when I'd sense my husband get frustrated because while I felt he saw it as obsessive and not fair, I only heard one thing: "Survive, Airam." Everything else was nonexistent. I saw nothing else. Remember how your body is a temple? I became unyielding and ruthless in doing whatever

I needed to do without question to survive. You know why? Because I was desperate to be on this planet to spend time with who? My husband. I'd get angry because I'd say to myself, "How does he not see I'm doing this so I can be here with him?" I'd translate it as, "He doesn't care, he doesn't get it." My heart would break, and then I'd get resentful. Now we had two resentful and afraid people just trying to survive, and "Vegan Veronica" with every diet stipulation, natural remedy, meditation app, and paranoia, who seemingly doesn't party, meeting my husband for the first time.

I'm a lot looser and have a new normal with a more wholesome balanced approach now, but hey, times were real then. I didn't want to change our lifestyle like that unannounced. I, too, wished I could go out as usual with friends and pretend I felt social. I, too, wanted to feel any ounce of normality. I was also grieving my lost identity being thrown into a new one; wishing my life could just go back to how it was and how I imagined it. I wished I could have the same regular fun. None of my life was normal at this point.

In many ways, God was creating newness, and I clung on. I didn't have a choice in that, but my choice was to survive. My biggest motivators were a sheer will to live, the purpose I believed God placed on my life to fulfill, and my husband. We had no clue how to navigate this crazy situation or communicate effectively between each other in such high stakes. (*And hello, can you imagine communication only one year into marriage? Communication grows with years, people.*

We're still learning!) As my response, I'd just go back to what I knew how to do best: Go into military mode. I told myself, "Sacrifice now Airam. Do whatever it takes to make sure you are here and as long as you're still here, the rest can be figured out later." I was so obsessively dedicated because I felt this intense pressure that if I didn't do my best, then I didn't do my best for him or my family, and I didn't honestly give my body the best shot I could have.

I put so much weight on myself out of the pure, sheer, painful will to be here. While my husband saw this as pushing him and our ordinary life away, I saw it as the only physical thing I knew to do to spend more time with him out of my love. There were so many honest, good-willed mixed signals. I encouraged myself to focus. And, although I painfully watched it take its toll at some moments, God told me to leave everything to Him, and so I did. We can't figure it all out ourselves. In just this one instance, do you see how we both went into our survival modes? Deep down in my core, I wasn't trying to disrespect his portion of the life we build or all the sacrifices he made. And deep down, he didn't want to make me feel unloved. When you look at the root, here's what you will find:

- We both were doing our best.
- We both did the only things we felt would be best.
- We both wanted me to be here.
- We were both trying to serve the other person.

It just got translated entirely differently from different perspectives.

How is this happening in your relationships in your life while in survival mode? Now, I'm sure you know me by now. I don't want to subscribe to all the ways things are going wrong, how people are letting you down, and how you feel you are coming short. Don't dwell here. Shift. Strategize your mental move and commit to one thing: "We are on the same team, and we are all doing the best we can in this present time." And take it one step further to learn from my experience. How can you look at things from another person's perspective?

I can guarantee the frustration is coming from a source of fear. And it's okay and understandable. You need to remember, the enemy isn't going to just move to the side and let you have an easy win; he comes at every angle. Even though you have the world on your plate, you still need to cover your home with prayer because I will tell you something. You nor anyone in your immediate circle have all the answers and know how to perfectly keep it together and flawlessly. So, here's what I want you to do: Be patient, be open to perspective, and be open to understanding. Focus on the communication. Always, always, always come from a place of love. No matter what. Dedicate your energy to love and respecting where they are. Remember, it is not you versus them; it is your family versus the enemy. When you don't have the wisdom or strength to do this, take it to God, and ask Him to take over. As much as you need your family, they need you too. As much as you are hurting, they are hurting in their own way. As much as you're doing your best, deep down, they are too. You may be thinking, "How can I pray for my family when I can barely pray for myself and all my needs."

Simply put in tough love: you've got to rise above. You are a champion. Do you know how you're going to carry it? Because you're not the only one carrying it. Jesus will take your unbearable load because He carried the cross He died on for you. For your burdens. For your healing. For your family. He's going to supernaturally guide you when you ask for help on how to navigate together. And remember to recruit others to pray. I am rooting for your team. You guys can do this, and you are not alone! God comforts and empowers us through Matthew 18:20: "For where two or three gather in my name, I am there among them." He's there.

Healing The Body Through Visualization

Visualization is one of my favorite things to pass forward as a secret weapon and tried-and-true method I used throughout my experience. I still use it to this day in many different areas of my life now. My dreams, goals, emotional healing, physical health, you name it. When I would pray for my body and talk to it in terms of the frequency it needed to be on, I started to develop methods at doing this. Like I've talked about earlier within the book, our thoughts and words are things. They shape every part of ourselves and what we see manifest in our lives. They have the power to shape the blessings we receive, and some we don't. The belief is the key part. "You of little faith...why (do) you doubt?" (Matthew 14:31) What do we do in times when we don't fully believe yet? We intentionally spend time with the Lord, in the word, or our discomfort until we move to a faith frequency.

There would be days that I would be meditating and praying over my body, and I would force myself to sit there for sometimes hours. One time, it was eight hours. I didn't have it in me to get up and wouldn't allow myself to do so until I genuinely in my spirit and heart believed what I was saying. You might call this torture; I call it discipline to win. Do you have to sit for eight hours? No. But I encourage you to sit and keep coming back to that meeting post with God until you move out of your doubt. And, it was really the only thing I knew to do. Sometimes, there would be an outburst of tears because I was frustrated that I didn't believe my words and thoughts.

I wanted to get up. I wanted to say, "This is stupid." But instead, I'd sit there and lovingly encouraging myself to say it louder even with my tears. I'd declare who I was. I'd declare who God was. I'd declare what His promises state from the Bible. Then I'd declare over my body and start again. I was ruthless. And, with enough shedding of myself and more opening myself to God, I'd start to believe it little by little. I'd start to feel confidence and peace with the declarations rather than anxiety and frustration. By the end, I'd feel joy. Then, and only then, would I get up. Over time, the hours slimmed down to minutes, and soon I had enough faith that I believed it on my own throughout the day. It became all I knew. I was equipped when opposing thoughts came in.

When declaring over my body, I went down to every detail. I went down to the fiber of my genetic make-up. God created me with a vivid and lively imagination. One day, when praying over my body, I imagined going inside my body through my prayer. I went inside, and I'd move from one area to the other, and it was like I could sense the state it was in. I could see it and feel it down to the vibration. I'd envision my genes beautifully changing like a Rubik's Cube: The bad ones turning off and the good ones turning on. I'd go inside and talk to the cells in my body and cover them with love and health. I'd imagine them growing abundant flowers and greenery while exuding vibrant colors, like bursts of paint at a Color Run or Holi festival. I'd tell myself that every cell was radiating healing, love, and joy; That every cell in my body was healthy. I would imagine my immune system as lush color that was full of life and capability, slowly moving through my body like the smoke of a blown-out candle; the same way the Holy Spirit moved through my body to see why I wanted to live. My body became this lively, bright, and strong environment that was bustling with lush activity.

What I didn't realize at the time of doing this was that this was an actual method people around the world had been using. I went to a church conference and got given a book by Dr. David Yonggi Cho by God's will. One of the speakers gave away copies of various books to attendees. The speaker didn't talk about healing at all. Still, within this book and Dr. David

Yonggi's story, I read about miraculous healing that started within himself and later, his family members. They attributed all of these to God. God sent me a grace capsule that took over me after reading that, and a lightbulb turned on. I started to look online for people who had done the same thing I was doing.

Come to find, there were countless studies and testimonies of people healing their bodies through prayer, meditation, and strategized visualization—hundreds, if not more. People had been doing this for years and years by changing their belief, channeling their inner frequencies, and accessing a healing realm most humans have no clue they have access to. I know it sounds all "woo-woo" at first. But I've witnessed it myself. I never knew it was possible; I was just going where my instinct and God lead me and later found validation that this was a method people weren't new to. I remember, after frantically seeing one after the other, I stopped, smiled, and leaned back in my chair. "Holy crap, this is a real thing."

Doctors even report better results in people in tune with their faith, mindfulness, and meditation. Another one of my favorite authors, who writes about this is Louise Hay. A doctor once told me a story of terminal children with the C-word and the doctors' last attempt at healing with no medicine alternatives because nothing worked. They had the children practice visualizing going into their bodies and pretending they were Star Wars characters or superheroes taking out the bad guys, sickness, and bad cells. She told me that ten or so out of twelve kids made a recovery.

I encourage you to try this. Try visualizing going into your body and seeing healing within your cells, on a specific body part, in your immune, or maybe it's an area in your life like your finances, marriage, home, or dream. Do this on an intentional and consistent basis. Visualize with your creativity and imagination how your body is working and healing for your good. Is the C-word, another ailment, or a different matter in your life an ice cube slowly melting away? Is God's light traveling through your body? Are your good cells carrying your bad cells out like an ant line? Is there a superhero that's wrangling up all the bad cells? Is your immune system a healthy flowing river that has a brilliant ecosystem running through your body? It's entirely up to you! Just avoid violence as a means of getting rid of the bad. Power is in your mind, and what you see can be.

I am praying for you.

I do hope with every fiber that whether you are going through the C-word or not, that you unlock all the miracles God professes already done in your life.

Thank you for being a part of mine and helping me share who He is. You will forever be a part of my purpose.

Let us use our time well. "Friends, don't get me wrong: By no means do I count myself an expert in all of this, but I've got my eye on the goal, where God is beckoning us onward—to Jesus. I'm off and running, and I'm not turning back." Philippians 3:14 MSG.

Airam Batdorf

AKB

I look forward to connecting with you on our website at **www.airambatdorf.com** for many resources to dive deeper into your faith while seizing every day to the fullest! To your victory.

Made in the USA
Columbia, SC
10 October 2020